Piero Sraffa

This is a lively intellectual biography of a leading protagonist of twentieth-century culture and his relations with other protagonists such as Gramsci, Keynes and Wittgenstein. The book includes an authoritative interpretation of his main work, *Production of Commodities by Means of Commodities*, a survey of the debates which followed its publication, and hence of the subsequent research strategies undertaken by different 'Sraffian schools'.

Piero Sraffa is not only one of the greatest economists of the twentieth century; he also exerted important influences on politics and philosophy through his friendship with the Italian communist leader Gramsci and the Austrian philosopher Wittgenstein. His economics moved away from the dominant marginalist tradition towards the rediscovery of classical political economy, revisited by ensuring internal consistency and openness to Keynesian views.

This book documents Sraffa's intellectual biography, his economic thought and the post-Sraffian developments.

Alessandro Roncaglia is Professor of Economics, University of Rome 'La Sapienza'.

Routledge Studies in the History of Economics

Piero Sraffa

His life, thought and
cultural heritage

Alessandro Roncaglia

London and New York

First published 2000
by Routledge
11 New Fetter Lane, London EC4P 4EE

Simultaneously published in the USA and Canada
by Routledge
29 West 35th Street, New York, NY 10001

Routledge is an imprint of the Taylor & Francis Group

Typeset in Sabon by
HWA Text and Data Management, Tunbridge Wells
Printed and bound in Great Britain by
TJ International Ltd, Padstow, Cornwall

British Library Cataloguing in Publication Data
A catalogue record for this book is available
from the British Library

Library of Congress Cataloging-in-Publication Data
A catalog record for this book has been requested

ISBN 0-415-23480-8

Contents

Introduction

Piero Sraffa (1898–1983) is generally held to be one of the leading intellectual figures of the twentieth century: not only for his direct contributions to economics, but also for his influence on other protagonists of European culture, such as Antonio Gramsci and Ludwig Wittgenstein.

Sraffa's role in the field of economic sciences has received contrasting evaluations. On the one hand, we have the extraordinary interest that his analyses aroused in so many economists all around the world, epitomised by Paul Samuelson's (1971: 400) reference to 'This age of Leontief and Sraffa'; let us note that Samuelson is not a follower of Sraffa's ideas, but one of the leading exponents of the system of thought criticised by the Italian economist. On the other hand, today's mainstream economists show a widespread feeling of impatience for Sraffian analysis: too frequently they leave aside the criticisms raised by Sraffa concerning the very foundations of their approach, and declare his contributions to be overrun by the most recent theoretical investigations; but do not explain why those criticisms can be disregarded.

Indeed, a full understanding of Sraffa's contributions can be difficult, since these must be viewed as a complex whole, as part of an extremely ambitious cultural project: 'to shunt the car of economic science' in a direction opposite to that – the subjective theory of value – chosen by Jevons, one of the leading early exponents of the marginalist approach.

Thus, with his writings Sraffa contributes to exposing the weak points in the theories of the leading exponents of the marginalist approach, from Alfred Marshall and Arthur Cecil Pigou to Friedrich von Hayek, and of their present-day followers, and at the same time re-proposes the classical approach of Adam Smith and David Ricardo (and also, in certain respects, of Karl Marx). The work of reconstructing the classical approach is also coherent with elements of the Keynesian contribution. This connection is possibly the most important issue in the current debate concerning the road to be followed in going on with the work started by Sraffa.

All these issues are discussed in the following pages. The three chapters consider respectively: a reconstruction of Sraffa's intellectual biography, and hence a first illustration of his complex cultural project and of the interactions between Sraffa and other protagonists of the cultural life of the twentieth century; an interpretation of his main work, *Production of Commodities by Means of Commodities* (Sraffa, 1960); a synthetic survey of the different streams of the lively debate aroused by the publication of that book, namely a survey of the different streams of research developed by the different 'Sraffian schools'. Trying to offer a sufficiently brief presentation of such wide issues implies that occasionally, especially in chapter III, the exposition is limited to brief hints accompanied by the appropriate bibliographical references. This explains the size of the bibliography, that anyhow constitutes only a fraction of the mass of writings available on the issues discussed in the present book.

The three chapters draw on previous writings. Specifically, Chapter 1 is a new version of an item 'Sraffa' written in 1994 for the *Enciclopedia del XX secolo* projected by the Istituto dell'enciclopedia italiana Treccani but as yet unpublished; Chapter 2 derives from papers presented at conferences on Sraffa held in Turin in October 1998 and in Rome in December 1998; Chapter 3 is a largely revised version of an essay on 'The Sraffian schools' published in a volume edited by Giacomo Becattini, *Il pensiero economico: temi, problemi e scuole* (Utet, Torino 1990). An attempt has been made to eliminate repetitions, leaving them only to the extent necessary to allow an independent reading of each chapter – though the three chapters complement each other, dealing with different aspects of a single theme.

The ideas illustrated in the following pages have been developed during a rather long stretch of time, since the writing of my degree dissertation defended in 1969, and through various publications, among which I recall in particular my book on *Sraffa and the Theory of Prices* (1975 in Italian, 1978 in English). I have discussed these ideas with too many persons – teachers, colleagues and friends, starting with Paolo Sylos Labini and Piero Sraffa – to be able now to recall all of them here; while giving shape to the present book, I received useful comments from Marcella Corsi, Nerio Naldi and Mario Tonveronachi; the index of names has been prepared by Silvia Brandolin.

In preparing this English edition, I benefited from Ian Steedman's comments, as well as from the comments of two anonymous referees: as a result, the English edition is a somewhat modified, slightly expanded, version of the original Italian one. The usual caveat applies: having accepted only part of the suggestions received, I am alone responsible for the final result. Finally, thanks are due to the Italian Ministry for universities and scientific research for financial support (research project on 'The historical archives of Italian economists').

Chapter 1

Piero Sraffa

The early writings: money and banking

Piero Sraffa was born in Turin on 5 August 1898. His father, Angelo Sraffa, was a well-known professor of commercial law and subsequently – for many years – dean of the Bocconi University in Milan. His father's career implied moving from one university to another; thus the young Sraffa began elementary school in Parma, to continue his education in Milan and Turin. Here he attended the secondary school, specialised in classical studies and went on to enrol in the faculty of Law. His attendance was by no means assiduous (in particular he shunned the lectures of Achille Loria (1857–1943), holder of the chair in political economy, who inspired him with little respect or liking). In fact, he spent 1917–20 doing his military service, and at the end of the war was assigned to the secretariat of the 'Royal Commission for the Investigation of Violations of Human Rights Committed by the Enemy', which concluded with the seven volumes of reports published between late 1919 and early 1921. He was thus able to take his exams in uniform, a condition which used to gain the favourable attention of the examiners. In November he graduated with a thesis on *Monetary Inflation in Italy during and after the War*. The supervisor of the thesis was Luigi Einaudi (1874–1961), a liberal senator since 1919 who was to become president of the Italian Republic; Sraffa remained on friendly terms with him for the rest of his life. However, the subject seems to have been suggested by Attilio Cabiati (1872–1950), who was professor of economics at Genoa at the time, and a friend of his father.[1]

The graduate thesis was also his first publication (Sraffa, 1920). A sharp rise in prices was associated with expansion in the circulation of money, in line with the dominant tradition of the quantity theory of money. Nevertheless, Sraffa's empirical analysis here stood at a distance from the quantity theory of money to consider pragmatically the differentiated trends shown by the various price indexes, their significance being sought in the different points of view of the various groups playing a part in economic life, and in particular the social classes of workers and entrepreneurs. The point is worth stressing, since it is precisely the non-univocal nature of the concept of the general price level (and thus of its inverse, the purchasing power of money) that underlies Keynes' criticism of the quantity theory of money in the opening chapters of his *Treatise on Money* (Keynes, 1930).

The most significant original contribution offered by Sraffa's thesis lies in the distinction between stabilisation of the internal and of the external value of money, or in other words between stabilisation of the average level of domestic prices and stabilisation of the exchange rate. According to traditional gold standard theory the two coincide, but in principle at least they should be kept apart. In fact, the distinction becomes essential both when considering short-term problems and inconvertible paper money systems; thus it was of crucial importance in the economic policy decision-making of the time.[2] Moreover, the point also has connections with the development of Keynesian theory: while Keynes made no use of the distinction in *Indian Currency and Finance* (1913), he did bring it into his *Tract on Monetary Reform* (1923), having in the meantime (in August, 1921) met Sraffa (who was to edit the Italian edition of the *Tract*).[3]

Sraffa's earliest publications continued to address monetary issues: an article of 1922 on the crisis of the Banca

Italiana di Sconto in the *Economic Journal*, and one on the bank crisis in Italy – again of 1922 – in the *Manchester Guardian Supplement on Reconstruction in Europe* edited by Keynes. The two articles reveal a thorough command of the institutional and technical aspects of banking (probably thanks in part to the practical experience the young Sraffa acquired in a provincial branch of a bank immediately after graduating), a strikingly well informed approach and awareness of the interests at stake.

The first of the articles reconstructs the story of the Banca Italiana di Sconto from its birth at the end of 1914 to bankruptcy in December, 1921. Sraffa concludes with some pessimistic remarks on the risks involved in direct relations between banks and enterprises and the inevitability of such relations given the backwardness of Italy's financial markets. He also comments on the difficulty of bringing about any change in the situation, due in the first place to a lack of real will at the political level. New laws are called for, he argues, 'to prevent the formation of trusts, to protect the independence of banks, to regulate the reserves on banking deposits', though in other countries' experience legislative reforms by themselves have shown to be insufficient to prevent crises. In Italy the risks are enhanced by the connections between the fascist government and the financial élite, as Sraffa stresses in a strong-worded final sentence:

> But even if these laws were not futile in themselves, what could be their use as long as the Government is prepared to be the first to break them so soon as it is blackmailed by a band of gunmen or a group of bold financiers?
>
> (Sraffa, 1922: 197)

All these points remain extremely relevant, often cropping up in the recent debates on the choice between the 'specialised' banking system (based on separation between short and medium-long term credit) and the 'universal' banking system that have marked the process of elaboration and ratification of the new Italian bank-law of 1993. Sraffa's attacks to the perverse connections between top politicians and financiers have also proved their persisting relevance on a number of occasions in recent years, such as in the bankruptcies of Sindona's Banca Privata Italiana (1974) and Calvi's Banco Ambrosiano (1983).

The second article highlights the weakness of Italy's three leading commercial banks (Banca Commerciale, Credito Italiano, Banca di Roma), casting serious doubts on the correctness of their official accounts and of the institutional expedient (resorting to a Consortium for industrial stock subsidies) adopted to side-step the law setting limits on the support issuing banks could give to commercial banks.

The first article, published in an academic journal, went unnoticed in Italian political and financial circles. The second article, however, was soon noticed and signalled to Mussolini who, strongly irritated and possibly worried by the impact the article could have on international financial circles in the presence of impending risks of a banking crisis, tele-graphed Angelo Sraffa demanding – to no avail – a public recantation from his son. The Banca Commerciale also threatened to sue, but took the threat no further. Its chair-man, Toeplitz, wrote a letter of protest to Keynes, as editor of the *Manchester Guardian Supplement*, who published it in a subsequent number with a short and harsh rejoinder. Given these circumstances, Keynes decided to invite the young Italian economist to Cambridge. Sraffa accepted, but was turned back when he landed at Dover in January 1923, possibly as a tribute by the British authorities to the Fascist government, possibly because Sraffa had already been branded *persona non grata* on account of the relations he had entered into with the British Marxist left on his previous visit of 1921.[4]

Monetary issues were subsequently to re-emerge among Sraffa's interests. A brief, biting attack on an article in *Popolo d'Italia* on the exchange rate movements of the lira was published in Piero Gobetti's (1901–26) *Rivoluzione liberale* in 1923; two letters on the revaluation of the lira were published by Angelo Tasca (1892–1960) in *Stato operaio* in 1927; from 1928 to 1930 he held courses in Cambridge on the Italian and German financial systems, along with his more celebrated courses on the theory of value. The 1932 controversy with Hayek, to which we shall return, was also about problems of monetary theory.

All in all, Sraffa's early publications show us a 'complete' economist, whose interest in pure theory is tempered by a solid knowledge of institutional details and exemplary analyses of specific real-world issues.

Friendship with Gramsci[5]

In 1919, at the University of Turin, Sraffa met Antonio Gramsci (1891–1937). They were introduced by Umberto Cosmo (1868–1944), who had been Sraffa's Italian teacher at upper secondary school; subsequently he went on to teach at the university, with Gramsci as one of his most brilliant students. In 1919 Gramsci founded *L'ordine nuovo* (The new order), and Sraffa collaborated with some translations from German and three short articles which he sent from London on the occasion of his visit there in 1921. The same year of 1921 saw the foundation of the Italian Communist Party in Livorno. Gramsci became its secretary in 1924. Sraffa never joined the party, maintaining independent views while keeping up a close intellectual relationship with his friend.

An important piece of evidence documenting the two friends' political exchanges is offered by a letter from Sraffa that Gramsci published (unsigned, initialled S.) in the April 1924 issue of *L'ordine nuovo* with his reply (Gramsci and Sraffa, 1924). In his letter Sraffa stressed the function played by bourgeois forces of opposition in the struggle against fascism and the importance of democratic institutions for the social and political development of the proletariat. In a scenario dominated by the rise of a fascist dictatorship, he found the working class absent from the political scene and the unions and communist party incapable of organising political action, while the workers had to face their problems as individuals, rather than as organised groups.

> The main issue, taking first place over any other, is one of 'freedom' and 'order': the others will come later, but for now they can be of no interest to the workers. Now is the time for the democratic forces of opposition, and I think we must let them act and possibly help them.

Antonio Gramsci's response was flatly negative, in line with the position of Amadeo Bordiga, then secretary of the communist party (where the centralist principle prevailed and no dissent to the official line could be shown). Gramsci rejected Sraffa's suggestions as conducive to the liquidation of the communist party, subjected as it would be to the strategy of the bourgeois forces of opposition, and went as far as accusing his friend of 'having so far failed to rid himself of the ideological residue of his liberal–democrat intellectual background, namely normative and Kantian, not Marxist and dialectical'. However, Gramsci's thesis – that the communist party should advance 'its own, autonomous solutions to the general, Italian problems' – did not in itself contradict the idea of an alliance for action with the other antifascist parties: an idea that Gramsci could never openly assert, since it differed from the party line.

Nevertheless, the very fact that Sraffa's letter was published, probably after heart-searching discussion between the two friends, amounted to significant recognition of the problems it raised and the political ideas suggested by the young economist. Indeed, Gramsci drew attention to these ideas again, far more explicitly, in a letter reserved for comrades closer to his position, and thus less subservient to the Bordiga orthodoxy (see Togliatti, 1962: 242 ff.).

The episode suggests that Sraffa played some role in the development of Gramsci's political thinking and the distance he took from Bordiga's line, in particular from the idea of the total opposition of the communist party to all the other political forces for the sake of the Bolshevik revolution. Years later, the point of arrival of Gramsci's political reflections appeared close to the position Sraffa had taken up as early as 1924, when Gramsci in turn proposed a pact between the anti-fascist political forces for the reconstruction of a democratic Italy after the hoped-for fall of the fascist regime. Indeed, we may see a particular significance in the fact that, apparently in their last meeting in March 1937,[6] it was to Sraffa that Gramsci entrusted a verbal message for the comrades still enjoying freedom, and one he attached great importance to – the watchword for the constituent assembly, encapsulating his proposal for a collaboration of the Italian communist party with all democratic, anti-fascist, forces.

Along with this fundamental point in the political debate, we must also recall the help Sraffa gave Gramsci after his arrest in 1926. It was he who took pains to get books and magazines to his friend in prison; it was he who explored the possible paths to freedom (on the binding condition that Gramsci insisted on, and which Sraffa adhered to, that no concessions be made to Fascism, such as a petition for pardon would imply); it was he who liaised with the communist leaders in exile and gave Gramsci further food for thought (through his sister-in-law Tatiana) in the reflections that were to take shape in the *Quaderni del carcere*. Some documentation of these activities can now be found in a posthumously published volume of letters from Sraffa to Tatiana (Sraffa, 1991).

Sraffa's friendship with Gramsci is an indication of an intense passion for politics which must be borne in mind to understand the ideological roots of the research project that Sraffa was to pursue in the field of economic science. It should, however, be emphasised that Sraffa's economic research and its results must be judged independently of his political background. It would not even seem as if Gramsci had any influence on the gradual switch in Sraffa's interests from problems of applied economics to theoretical ones in the first half of the 1920s.

Criticism of Marshallian theory [7]

Thus, in the years following his graduation Sraffa's interests ranged from politics to questions of applied economics, and in particular – but not only – monetary economics.

After his brief experience as a bank clerk Sraffa spent a year in London attending courses at the London School of Economics. He was then appointed director of the Labour Office of the Milan Provincial Council, at the time under the socialist administration presided over by a lawyer, Nino Levi, who was however soon to resign when the fascist regime took over and the socialist provincial council fell.

It was then that Sraffa turned to an academic career, which he began as lecturer on political economy and public finance in the University of Perugia, Faculty of Law. Sraffa had probably read at least some of the works of Marx and the major classical and marginalist economists before 1923, but the evidence suggests that his interest in theoretical problems – possibly stimulated during his 1921–22 stay in London – developed at this stage, and deepened when he took on a general course in political economy.[8] He then found himself having to confront the academic framework then dominant in Italy, namely marginalism in the Marshallian version of Maffeo Pantaleoni (1857–1924), whom Sraffa (1924: 648) himself called 'the prince of [Italy's] economists'.

In fact,[9] keeping faith with the principle he often recommended to his students (always look to the best exponent of the approach to be criticised), Sraffa adopted for his lessons Marshall's *Principles* which, although conceived as a reference book for university courses, was by no means the simplest textbook that students of a law faculty could wish for.

The fruits of Sraffa's reflections – a radical critique of the Marshallian theory of the equilibrium of the firm and the industry – were set out in a long article published in 1925 in the *Annali di economia* entitled 'On the relations between cost and quantity produced'. Five years had passed since publication of the eighth edition of Marshall's *Principles of Economics*, and one year since his death.

Sraffa's article was a contribution to the debate on the 'laws of returns' sparked off by a paper that John Harold Clapham (1873–1946) published in the *Economic Journal* in 1922. The point in question was of vital importance for the Marshallian theoretical construction and, more generally speaking, for the marginalist theory of value.

According to the marginalist approach, prices are to be seen as indexes of relative scarcity; the equilibrium values for prices and quantities produced are determined through a confrontation between the preferences of economic agents and the scarcity of available resources, and thus by the balancing of demand and supply. A decisive factor in this approach and, in particular, in the Marshallian method of partial equilibria – where the market for each single commodity is analysed in isolation – is the plotting of a supply curve for each product expressing the (marginal) cost as a function of the quantity produced, both for the individual firm and for the industry as a whole.

Marshallian theory singles out three cases accounting for all eventualities: constant, increasing or decreasing returns, according to whether the average unit cost remains constant, decreases or increases when the quantity produced increases. Clapham, a professor of economic history, set out to tackle the problem of the concrete application of these theoretical categories, and came to a startling conclusion, finding the theoretical apparatus in question sterile: the three categories of constant, increasing and decreasing costs were 'empty economic boxes' (this was also the title of his paper), impossible to fill with concrete examples of real industries.

Clapham's article provoked immediate response, with an article in the following issue of the *Economic Journal* by Arthur Cecil Pigou (1877–1959), Marshall's successor to the chair of economics at the University of Cambridge and paladin of a line in Marshallian orthodoxy that led to the 'geometrical method' of demand and supply curves for the firm and the industry, for the short and the long period. This construct, it should be noted, does not fully correspond to Marshall's view of the matter; tacking between ambiguities, constantly veering back en route, in subsequent editions of the *Principles* Marshall had attempted to reconcile an evolutionist, and thus intrinsically dynamic, conception with an analytic apparatus based on conditions of demand and supply equilibrium, and thus necessarily static.[10] A greater fidelity to Marshall's ideas was in fact shown by Dennis Robertson (1890–1963), who raised further doubts on Pigou's analytic apparatus in an article published in the March 1924 issue of the *Economic Journal*.

The debate continued in the pages of the *Economic Journal*, unflagging after the publication of Sraffa's articles (the Italian article of 1925 and another article, published in the December, 1926 *Economic Journal*, which we shall be dealing with subsequently), with contributions by Allyn Young, Pigou, Lionel Robbins, Joseph Schumpeter, Roy Harrod and, in 1930, with a symposium on 'Increasing Returns and the Representative Firm' with Robertson, Shove and Sraffa as protagonists.

Clearly, it was a 'battle of giants', largely fought out in an outstanding arena, the economists' major academic periodical of the time. It is all the more odd, therefore, that its conclusions have been systematically ignored in economics textbooks ever since, the trend being set by Paul Samuelson's highly successful *Economics* (over two million copies sold in various languages from 1948 to the present day), as if the theoretical debate held no implications for the parables used in the education of students, even when their erroneousness is evident to all.

Sraffa joined in the debate Clapham had begun by arguing that the problem of the 'empty boxes' was not a matter of applying the theoretical categories of constant, increasing and decreasing returns to real situations, but laid rather in the insurmountable difficulties encountered in the theory of firm and industry equilibrium. Underlying all this, Sraffa pointed out, was a conceptual confusion: in classical political economy the 'law' of decreasing returns was associated with the problem of rent (theory of distribution), while the 'law' of increasing returns was associated with the division of labour, or in other words general economic progress (theory of production). Marshall and other neo-classical economists had tried to put these two 'laws' on the same plane, co-ordinating them in a single 'law of non-proportional returns' with the aim of expressing costs as a function of the quantity produced, for firm and industry alike. These functions were then applied in the theory of prices, transformed into supply curves for the various products to be set against the corresponding demand curves obtained by applying the 'law' of decreasing marginal utility (where, as Marshall noted, the demand and supply curves may be each compared with one of the blades of a pair of scissors). However, this means transposing increasing and decreasing returns to an ambit different from the original ones; and this fact makes it difficult to apply in the new ambit the justifications originally used to account for cost trends. Sraffa illustrates these difficulties analysing the literature on the subject while focusing his attention on the long period.

In particular, Sraffa underlines the point that decreasing returns have to do with changes in the proportions of factors of production, while increasing returns are associated with expanding production and increasing division of labour.

The former case – decreasing returns – occurs when a factor of production proves scarce. Now, unless we identify the industry with all the firms using a scarce factor, the variations in average cost associated with increased production in the industry in question will be of the same order of magnitude as the variations in costs experienced by the other industries using the same production factor. Here we have a clear violation of the *ceteris paribus* condition underlying the Marshallian analysis of partial equilibria.

In the case of increasing returns, they cannot be present in both the industry and the firms within it at the same time, since otherwise the firms would go on expanding, to transcend the limits of competition; nor can they be found in various industries at the same time, otherwise the *ceteris paribus* clause would be breached once again. It is only in the case of production economies external to the individual firms but internal to the industry that consistency is ensured between increasing returns, the assumption of competition and the partial equilibria method, but Sraffa rightly considers such a case unrealistic.[11] In conclusion, we may say that the analytic construct of the Marshallian tradition can only be made to square with the canons of logical coherence through unrealistic *ad hoc* hypotheses – hardly a sound basis for a framework designed for general interpretative application.

Imperfect competition

Sraffa's 1925 paper attracted the interest of Francis Ysidro Edgeworth (1854–1926), who was co-editor of the *Economic Journal* together with Keynes. Prompted by Edgeworth, Keynes asked Sraffa for an article to be published in the British periodical, and the young Italian economist was ready to accept the offer.[12]

The English paper (Sraffa, 1926) is much shorter than the Italian version, and correspondingly much less rich in collateral elements of noticeable importance: the first half of the article consists of a summary of the main points in the Italian article, while the second half elaborates an original line of research based on negatively sloped demand curves hypothesised also in the case of individual firms and thus compatible with constant or moderately increasing returns. Here we have a theory of imperfect competition which, in fact, takes up certain cues for 'realism' scattered through Marshall's work. However, Sraffa is quick to point out the limits to this line of research, remarking towards the conclusion 'that in the foregoing the disturbing influence exercised by the competition of new firms attracted to an industry the conditions of which permit of high monopolist profits has been neglected'. Basically, this meant neglecting competition in the classical sense of the term, consisting in the shifting of capital from one sector to another in pursuit of maximum returns.

In the following years the theory of imperfect competition was to prove a rich minefield. In particular, Joan Robinson (1933) elaborated a systematic treatment of the subject, while at the same time, with his theory of monopolistic competition, Edward Chamberlin (1933) offered an approach that had various points in common. However, while Robinson worked in the conceptual terms of Marshall's 'partial equilibria', developing a theory of imperfect competition regarding firms operating within a given industry, the confines between the various industries become somewhat blurred in Chamberlin's theory: each firm operates in its own market under the constraint of competition from outside, without any need to specify whether the competition comes from firms producing more or less the same commodity as the firm in question, or quite different products that might nevertheless serve sufficiently well in their place.

Although Sraffa's was the crucial first step behind this line of research (which still exerts a certain influence today and, above all, still finds its way into the textbooks: curiously enough,[13] it is perhaps to this that our Torinese economist owes most of his fame today, especially in the United States), he was soon to abandon it. As we have seen, it was based on a notion of competition – the notion the marginalist approach was to focus on, implying a large number of firms supplying an identical product – that departed radically from the classical economists' idea of free flows of capital between the various sectors of the economy. It was in fact the conclusion of Sraffa's 1926 paper that paved the way to the modern theory of non-competitive market forms, and in particular Paolo Sylos Labini's theory of oligopoly (1962), based on the presence of obstacles to the entry of new firms into the market. It was the classical notion of competition, furthermore, that constituted the basis for a line of research that Sraffa was already developing in a first draft, discussed with Keynes in 1928, and which was eventually to find expression in *Production of Commodities by Means of Commodities*.[14]

Criticism of the representative firm

Sraffa's radical departure from the traditional framework of the theory of the firm and the industry is evident in the last writings he dedicated to the subject, namely his contributions to the symposium on 'Increasing Returns and the Representative Firm' published in the *Economic Journal* of March 1930. In fact, the conclusion of Sraffa's brief contributions is clearcut, marking a frontal opposition to the received view: 'Marshall's theory [...] cannot be interpreted in a way which makes it logically self-consistent and, at the same time, reconciles it with the facts it sets out to explain;' thus 'I think [...] that [it] should be discarded'.[15]

It is worth noting that here Sraffa's criticism is directed against a version of Marshallian theory more faithful to Marshall's own original framework than Pigou's, namely the evolutionary version Robertson presented in his contribution to the symposium (Robertson, 1930) based on the concept of the firm's 'life cycle' which Marshall had employed in an attempt to make increasing returns compatible with the firm's competitive equilibrium. Like a biological organism, the firm goes through successive stages of development, maturity and decline, the 'representative' firm being half-way through the process of development and thus at a stage of increasing returns to scale. As Marshall himself pointed out, a concept of this type, that sees the expansion of firms depending on the 'life cycle' of entrepreneurial capacities can be contemplated in the case of directly family-run concerns, but could not apply to modern joint stock companies.[16]

Thus the biological analogy proved a false exit to the blind alley Marshallian analysis had got into, hemmed in by the contradiction between increasing returns and competitive equilibrium, and Sraffa was able to point up the *deus ex machina* nature of the biological metaphors that Robertson used following in Marshall's wake, and which could not fill in the gaps in logical consistency left by these analytic structures:

> At the critical points of his argument the firms and the industry drop out of the scene, and their place is taken by the trees and the forest, the bones and the skeleton, the water-drops and the wave – indeed all the kingdoms of nature are drawn upon to contribute to the wealth of his metaphors.
>
> (Sraffa, 1930: 90–1)

Cambridge

The 1926 paper published in the *Economic Journal* had considerable impact, especially in Cambridge, and Keynes had no difficulty in offering Sraffa a post as lecturer in the university which was then – and would remain for many years to come – the most prestigious centre for economic theory in the world. In 1926 Sraffa had also been awarded a chair in Italy, at Cagliari, but after Gramsci's imprisonment and the threats he himself had received as an anti-fascist,[17] he decided to move to England, where he was to live from 1927 until his death on 3 September, 1983.

Holding a teaching post in a prestigious foreign university, Sraffa retained his chair in Italy, passing his salary to the economics library of Cagliari University. When Italian professors were called upon to swear loyalty to fascism, Sraffa resigned,[18] wishing neither to take such an oath nor to dissociate himself from the line chosen by the communist party, which was to fulfil what might be seen as a purely formal obligation in order to keep channels of communication open with the younger generations (a line that meant a painful *volte-face* for the famous Latinist, Concetto Marchesi, a militant communist who took the oath after a public declaration that he never would).

After a year spent settling in (despite his previous stays in England, his English was by no means perfect when he arrived, his French and possibly even his German being better), Sraffa held courses in Cambridge on the theory of value and the German and Italian financial systems. His lessons caused something of a stir: Sraffa discussed the theories of the classical economists, Ricardo in particular, and the theories of general economic equilibrium expounded by Walras and Pareto – little of which were known in England – as well as advancing his own criticisms of the Cambridge (Marshall–Pigou) tradition, in particular the theory of the firm. However, Sraffa found himself increasingly fighting shy of speaking in public, and thus of giving lectures too; thanks to Keynes, he was then appointed director of research and subsequently head librarian of the Marshall Library, the library of the Economics faculty. On his arrival he entered King's College, the same college as Keynes, to become fellow of Trinity College in 1939 and remain there for the rest of his life.

In the cloistered calm of Cambridge, Sraffa developed his research along three lines connected in one great design: work on the critical edition of Ricardo's writings, entrusted to him by the Royal Society on the initiative of Keynes in 1930; research in the field of the theory of value, which was to culminate after thirty years' labour in *Production of Commodities by Means of Commodities* (in the Preface Sraffa recalls showing Keynes an outline of the central propositions as early as 1928); and a collateral interest in the development of Keynesian theory, in particular during the early 1930s. It was, moreover, at Cambridge that Sraffa made the acquaintance of the Austrian philosopher Ludwig Wittgenstein (1885–1951), who became a friend and on whom Sraffa was to have a significant influence.

In the following sections we shall be considering, in order, Sraffa's relations with Wittgenstein, those with Keynes, his interpretation of Ricardo and the classics, and the contribution offered by his 1960 volume. We will then focus, in turn, on the elements of reconstruction and development of the classical framework, and on those that constitute the 'premises' for a critique of marginalist theory. On this basis we may attempt to advance our own interpretation of the cultural design pursued by Sraffa.

Wittgenstein

Sraffa met Wittgenstein in 1926. The Austrian philosopher had just arrived in Cambridge, called there by Bertrand Russell who a few years before had Wittgenstein's *Tractatus Logico-Philsosophicus* (1922) published. The book constituted a fundamental contribution to the development of modern philosophy, and is considered by many to be the culmination of logical neo-positivism.

Wittgenstein had pondered and drafted it during the war, first on the Russian front, then on the Italian front, and finally during his brief period of imprisonment in Italy at the end of the war. Wittgenstein himself had conceived it as the terminus of philosophical research; having completed it, he considered that he had no other work to do in the philosophical field.

A difficult, withdrawn character, Wittgenstein retreated to teach in an Austrian small village primary school and to work as a monastery gardener. His contact with philosophical research was indeed scant: a few letters and the occasional meeting with Bertrand Russell or the young Frank Ramsey, another philosopher and mathematician of Cambridge who was also a friend of Sraffa's, and who died at the early age of 26 in 1930, but above all with the so-called Circle of Vienna whose moving spirit was Moritz Schlick.

It may well have been the Viennese discussions – and in particular a celebrated lecture Brouwer gave on the foundations of mathematics – that finally persuaded Wittgenstein that after all there remained some work to be done in the philosophical field. So it was that Wittgenstein arrived in Cambridge early in 1929, to become fellow of Trinity College after a few months and remain – with a few odd breaks – until his death in April 1951.

During the periods that found them both in Cambridge, Wittgenstein and Sraffa would in general spend one afternoon a week together, discussion ranging here and there rather than dwelling on philosophy or economics as such. However, their debates had a decisive influence on the Austrian philosopher, and on the transition from the logical atomism of the *Tractatus* to the mature positions emerging in the *Philosophical Investigations*, published posthumously in 1953.

Georg von Wright, a pupil of Wittgenstein, reports him as once having said 'that his discussions with Sraffa made him feel like a tree from which all the branches had been cut'.[19] Wittgenstein himself is still more explicit in his Preface to the *Philosophical Investigations*:

> I am indebted to [the criticism] which a teacher of this university, Mr. P. Sraffa, for many years unceasingly practised on my thoughts. I am indebted to *this* stimulus [the italics are Wittgenstein's] for the most consequential ideas of this book.

There is some disagreement among the specialists assessing relations between early and late Wittgenstein: some speak of continuity, others of a hiatus. My impression is that gradual as the change was, showing no sudden breakthrough, it nevertheless reached very deep.

With a drastic simplification, also leaving aside other by no means secondary aspects of Wittgenstein's thought, we may illustrate his position as follows.[20] The *Tractatus* argued a correspondence between the world and the elements that constitute it ('facts') on the one hand, and our representation of the world (whose constituent elements are 'thoughts', expressed in 'propositions') on the other. On this basis Wittgenstein argued that it is possible to build a logical, axiomatic set of propositions, each describing a 'fact' while together they describe the world, or rather, if not all the world, all that can be described in a rational form. Moreover, on that for which no rational description can be provided (sentiments, religious beliefs, aesthetic judgements, etc.), says Wittgenstein, 'one must be silent'.

However, in the *Philosophical Investigations* Wittgenstein abandons the idea of language as axiomatic representation of the world, and the idea of the 'unspeakable'. Discussions with Sraffa seem to have played their part in his abandonment of the latter. In this connection, there is an anecdote that Wittgenstein himself liked to tell his pupils, one of whom – Malcolm – recounts it thus in his biography of the master: one day, as they were travelling together on the train from Cambridge to London, 'Sraffa made a gesture, familiar to Neapolitans and meaning something like disgust or contempt, of brushing the underneath of his chin with an outward sweep of the finger tips of one hand'.[21]

The gesture can only acquire a specific meaning from the context in which it is performed, thus contradicting Wittgenstein's idea that every proposition had to have a precise place in the axiomatic order of rational language, independently of the various contexts in which it may be employed.[22]

In any case, in the *Philosophical Investigations* Wittgenstein develops a new theory of language and the relations between it and the world it should describe. There is not just one type of language, Wittgenstein asserts,

> but there are *countless* kinds: countless different types of use of what we call 'symbols', 'words', 'sentences'. And this multiplicity is not something fixed, given once for all; but new types of language, new language-games, as we may say, come into existence, and others become obsolete and get forgotten.

In general, Wittgenstein goes on, 'the meaning of a word is its use in the language'.[23] However, words do not correspond to simple elements of reality, and these simple elements cannot be defined; nor is it possible to produce a general theory of language. Wittgenstein demonstrated these theses with a series of examples of 'language games' – theoretical models focusing attention on particular aspects of the real language, presenting them as the general language of a group of people.

We shall be seeing later (Chapter 2) how the changes in Wittgenstein's philosophical position can be compared with the differences between the marginalist approach of general economic equilibrium and Sraffa's theoretical contribution. Here we have simply pointed out that the Austrian philosopher's initial position prompted some critical remarks from the Italian economist, which were to play an important role in Wittgenstein's subsequent thinking. We may perhaps detect Sraffa's political interests behind his opposition to an *a priori* theory of language, and his preference for a theory open to recognition of the role played by social factors (the environment within which the 'language game' takes place). In any case, although it is difficult to specify its precise nature given the insufficiency of the documentation, there can be no doubt that Sraffa had a significant influence on Wittgenstein's thinking, and thus also upon the course of contemporary philosophy.

Friendship with Keynes and the criticism of Hayek

After Gramsci and Wittgenstein, the third protagonist of twentieth-century culture to have fecund exchange with Sraffa was John Maynard Keynes, although this was a rather different case. In the first place, it came within Sraffa's own field of professional research, economics; secondly, while the evidence shows fruitful communication in both directions, it seems probable that Keynes – who was fifteen years older – played the major role.

Keynes was of great help to Sraffa on various occasions: it was he who asked Sraffa for a contribution for the *Manchester Guardian Supplement*, and who decided to publish the twenty-four-year-old Italian economist's 1922 paper in the prestigious *Economic Journal*. Again, it was Keynes who asked him – although acting on a suggestion of Edgeworth's

– for the paper criticising the Marshallian theory of the firm which came out in December 1926; he also called him to Cambridge, had the Royal Economic Society entrust him with the editing of the critical edition of Ricardo's *Works and Correspondence* and found him congenial roles such as director of research and librarian, as well as having him released from the detention camp Sraffa had been sent to as 'enemy alien' when Italy went to war. The only publication Sraffa signed jointly was with Keynes: both were keen bibliophiles, and in 1938 they edited the reprint of an extremely rare booklet, *An Abstract of a Treatise of Human Nature*, complete with a learned introduction containing decisive proof for its attribution to Hume rather than Adam Smith, as was generally supposed. Sraffa also took care of the Italian edition (1925) of Keynes' *Tract on Monetary Reform*, and played a primary role in stimulating the publication in Italian of other writings of the Cambridge economist.

More relevant to our immediate concern, however, was the cultural exchange in the field of economic theory. Four episodes deserve particular attention.

The first, referred to above, was the influence an idea developed by Sraffa in his graduate thesis may have had on Keynes, i.e. the distinction between the stabilisation of money in relation to the level of domestic prices and in relation to the exchange rate.

The second episode is recalled by Sraffa himself in his Preface to *Production of Commodities by Means of Commodities*, where he tells us that 'when in 1928 Lord Keynes read a draft of the opening propositions of this paper, he recommended that, if constant returns were *not* to be assumed, an emphatic warning to that effect should be given'. Keynes is the only economist to be thanked in the Preface (his thanks also go to three mathematicians – Ramsey, Watson and Besicovitch – and, in the Italian edition, to Raffaele Mattioli, a banker who long played a leading role in the Banca Commerciale Italiana as well as being a very close friend of Sraffa's and *magna pars* in the preparation of the Italian edition of the book). The point Keynes intervened on is of fundamental importance since – as we shall see more clearly in the next chapter – the absence of a hypothesis on returns constitutes a crucially distinctive feature of Sraffa's book, implying among other things abandonment of the marginalist conception of equilibrium. Thus it seems quite likely that his discussions with Keynes played an important role in the development of Sraffa's ideas.

The third episode concerns Sraffa's participation in the so-called Cambridge Circus: a group consisting of the best of Cambridge's young economists – including, along with Sraffa, Richard Kahn, who liaised with Keynes, James Meade, Austin and Joan Robinson – who discussed Keynes' *Treatise on Money* of 1930 and his ideas in the transitional phase between the *Treatise* and the *General Theory* (1936). However, the role played by the Cambridge Circus in the development of Keynes' ideas is far from settled, and it is still harder to pick out the particular contributions of individual members. From the debate material published in the Royal Economic Society edition of Keynes's *Collected Writings*, Sraffa's contributions do not appear particularly significant (see Keynes, 1973; 1979), but things may have been different.[24]

The fourth episode was the development of a tool for analysis, namely the own rates of interest that Keynes uses in chapter XVII of the *General Theory*. This analytic tool was proposed by Sraffa in an article published in the March 1932 issue of the *Economic Journal* which amounted largely to a markedly critical review of *Prices and Production* by Hayek (1931a). The following issue of the *Economic Journal* included a reply by Hayek (1932) and a brief rejoinder by Sraffa.

The review-article came just six months after the publication of Hayek's work – a reaction as prompt as it was severe, justified by the need to stress as drastically as possible the difference between the Keynesian analysis presented in the *Treatise on Money*[25] and Hayek's theory of money and cycle, which rests explicitly on the marginalist (or Austrian, to be more precise) apparatus of value theory. There was clearly the risk of an operation to re-absorb Keynes' analysis into the general current of traditional marginalism, much as was to be attempted by the exponents of the so-called neoclassical synthesis after the publication of the *General Theory*. The incisiveness of Sraffa's criticism of Hayek had a significant role in deepening, at least for a time, the abyss separating Keynes from the more rigorous versions of the marginalist tradition – i.e. the continental, and particularly the Austrian one.[26]

Hayek observes that 'monetary influences play a dominant role in determining both the volume and direction of production' (Hayek, 1931a: 1). For traditional marginalist analysis, on the other hand, 'at a condition of equilibrium [...] no unused resources exist' (1931a: 31), among other things because falls or rises in the interest rate bring about 'a transition to more or less "round-about" methods of production' (1931a: 33). The task Hayek sets himself is in fact to reconcile marginalist theory with reality. Of course, Hayek's analysis of the influence monetary factors have on the real variables cannot be a matter of 'static analysis' but only concerns 'fluctuations of production', 'to build on the foundations given by the concept of a tendency towards an equilibrium' (1931a: 31). In other words, Hayek elaborates an analysis of the 'dynamics of disequilibrium' with particular reference to situations where the 'monetary' rate of interest diverges from the 'natural' rate (as understood by Wicksell 1936), and to the effects of monetary perturbations on the relative prices of consumption goods and producer goods (see also Hayek, 1932: 238).

Hayek's analysis, with its theory of 'real' economic equilibrium, rests on the concept of 'period of production' and the thesis that the 'capital intensity' of production processes is a decreasing function of the interest rate. This thesis comes in for destructive criticism from Sraffa in chapters 6 and 12 of his 1960 book, but in the 1932 article his attention focuses on Hayek's monetary analysis.

By characterising monetary vicissitudes as causing disequilibrium in the system, Hayek brings attention to bear on the 'forced saving' brought about by the deviation of the market interest rate from the 'natural' interest rate. Thus he demonstrates how with sufficiently general hypotheses the capital accumulated through forced saving in the ascending phase of the cycle is economically destroyed in the descending phase, restoring the economy to its original equilibrium.

In his review Sraffa points out that Hayek's argument fails to take account of certain features typical of a monetary economy, where money is not only a means of payment but also a unit of measurement in contracts and a store of value (Sraffa, 1932: 421–43). It can therefore by no means be taken for granted that capital accumulated with forced saving will be economically destroyed through the play of actions and reactions of market automatism; in general the new capital will go towards bringing about a new state of equilibrium in the economic system.

Here Sraffa adds a further critical observation. When relative prices as a whole are not constant in the course of time, each commodity has its 'own interest rate'. This happens in phases of transition from one equilibrium to another, even in barter economies. Thus, apart from the highly unlikely case of invariance in technology or equiproportional variations, growth phases are characterised by the impossibility of defining *one* equilibrium interest rate, whether in barter or monetary economies. Hayek's answer on this count – that 'there might, at any moment, be as many "natural" interest rates as there are commodities, *all* of which would be *equilibrium rates*' (Hayek, 1932: 245) – may be taken as one of the first signs of the appearance of a new analytic concept, namely that of inter-temporal equilibrium (see Milgate, 1979).

We may well imagine Hayek's dismay faced with a position such as Sraffa's must have seemed to him. Here we are, in a world where monetary factors exert an evident influence on real variables, and where the marginalist theory of value is universally accepted. What, then, could the outcome possibly be of rejecting out of hand what seemed to be the only possible way to reconcile faithfulness to the theoretical foundations of marginalism with the realities of unemployment and cyclic trends in the economy? Today it appears quite clear to us that what to Hayek seemed like nihilism on Sraffa's side (much like the attitude shown towards Marshallian theory in the 1930 article) was simply rejection of the marginalist approach – not as a 'leap into the dark', but in favour of the reconstruction of political economy based on the alternative approach of the classical school.

The critical edition of Ricardo's writings

The difficulties economists like Hayek and Robertson had in understanding just what Sraffa was getting at (and, more generally speaking, the widespread impression of Sraffa as a 'critical spirit but not reconstructive') show the extent to which the marginalist approach had encroached on the classical tradition in the first half of the twentieth century, actually submerging it. Hence the goal Sraffa sets himself with the critical edition of Ricardo's works, namely to propose once again the framework the classical economists had created for political economy, which was also the framework Marx had taken up and developed.

Sraffa began work on Ricardo's writings in 1930, and went on with it for over a quarter of a century, while at the same time pressing ahead with the theoretical work that would lead to *Production of Commodities by Means of Commodities*.

Once again it was Keynes, in his capacity as secretary of the Royal Economic Society, who determined the assignment of editing the critical edition of Ricardo's *Works and Correspondence* to Sraffa and more than once, in the years to come, was to step in on behalf of a Sraffa harried by the publisher over delays in completing the work. Finally, it was with Keynes' help that Sraffa engaged in a painstaking manuscript hunt that was soon bearing fruit. As early as 1930 a chest containing the letters Ricardo received from his correspondents was found in the house of one of his heirs. On many other occasions the search proved fruitless, but Sraffa succeeded nevertheless in amassing a huge amount of material thanks to which he was able to fill out a richly detailed picture of Ricardo's cultural and human environment.

Then, in 1943, after thirteen years' research and with the six volumes ready in proof, a number of extremely important letters from Ricardo to James Mill were found in an Irish castle, together with various other manuscripts including the fundamental essay on 'Absolute value and exchangeable value' which Ricardo had been working on in the last weeks of his life.

For the final stages of work, with pressure from the Royal Society and the publisher mounting relentlessly, Sraffa was partnered in his labours with Maurice Dobb, a Marxist economist and one of his best friends. Keynes and Austin Robinson saw him as the only one who could stand up to the meticulousness and timetables (late into the night) of the Italian economist.[27] At last, between 1951 and 1955, the now ten volumes of the *Works and Correspondence* of David Ricardo made their appearance, to be followed in 1973 by a painstakingly compiled volume of indexes.

After a century of near oblivion and misleading interpretations, Sraffa's philological rigour plays a decisive role in the rediscovery of the classical economists' framework based on the surplus approach. When Sraffa began his work, let it be remembered, the most commonly accepted interpretations were those of Marshall (1961, Appendix i), who saw Ricardo as a – somewhat imprecise and limited – precursor of modern theory (in that he took account of the cost of production, i.e. supply, but not of demand in the determination of prices), and Jevons (in the Preface to the second edition of the *Theory of Political Economy*, 1879), who found Ricardo responsible for having perniciously diverted economics from the path of true science. From either interpretation, there was no reason to waste time on Ricardo's works.

This opinion was shared, for instance, by such distinguished economists as Robertson and Hicks, as their correspondence with Keynes reveals.[28] Acknowledgements extended, at the most, to the 'Ricardian' theory of rent as forerunner of the principle of decreasing marginal productivity, to Ricardo's theory of money and to his theory of international trade based on the principle of comparative costs. Nevertheless, expectations were stirring about Sraffa's work. Publication was signalled as imminent on a number of occasions – by Luigi Einaudi in *Riforma sociale* in 1931, by Keynes in his 1933 essay on Malthus, by Sraffa himself in a letter to Rodolfo Morandi in 1934. ... In his *History of Economic Analysis*, published posthumously in 1954, Schumpeter expresses the hope that 'Some day, perhaps, we may see the completion of Professor Sraffa's comprehensive edition of Ricardo's works, which we have been eagerly awaiting these twenty years'.[29]

Such expectations were more than justified. Sraffa's critical edition of Ricardo's *Works and Correspondence* is unanimously recognised as a model of philological rigour, and it was above all for this that in 1961 Sraffa was awarded the gold medal of the Swedish Academy of Science. Keynes and Myrdal also figured among the economists honoured with the medal, which anticipated the Nobel Prize for economics, awarded only as from 1969. The works published in this edition, together with the apparatus of notes and, above all, Sraffa's introduction to the first volume, restore Ricardo – and through him the whole school of classical political economy – to a central position in economic theory, freeing interpretation from the accretions of misleading marginalist readings.

Sraffa stresses the importance of the notion of the surplus, and of the conception of the economic system as a circular flow of production and consumption, which Ricardo inherited from an already robust school of thought: suffice it here to recall William Petty (1623–87) for the concept of surplus and François Quesnay (1694–1774) for the idea of the circular flow. Ricardo's 'political' interest in the corn laws and the limits they set to accumulation led him to construct a rigorous analytic structure with clear policy implications. In fact, such a structure throws into sharp relief the negative effects that obstacles to free trade have on profits and, through them, on investments. According to Sraffa's interpretation, at the outset (in the 1815 *Essay on the Influence of the Low Price of Corn on the Profits of Stock*) Ricardo implicitly relied on a simplified model (possibly set out in the lost 'Papers on the profits of capital') where a certain amount of corn used as means of production (seeds and subsistence wage for the workers engaged in the productive process) would yield a greater amount of corn. With the initial supplies of means of production and subsistence reconstituted, a surplus thus remains that accrues to the owning classes (as profit to the capitalists, and as rent to the land-owners). Should the land show varying degrees of fertility, then the result of competition between the farmers to rent the best lands from the landowners will be a rent paid for these lands. Such rents will be determined by the difference between the unit cost of production each plot of land entails and the corresponding cost for the worst lands under cultivation.[30] As the population increases, less and less fertile lands must be brought under cultivation: the cost of wheat obtained on the worst of the lands under cultivation rises and profit thus falls while the rents on the other lands increase, the real wage remaining unchanged at subsistence level. The rate of profits will also diminish. In fact, in the simplified system Ricardo considers, it can be determined as the ratio between two physical magnitudes of the same commodity: the quantity of corn that goes to the capitalists as profit, and the quantity of corn advanced by the capitalists as means of production. The 'competition of capitals' ensures that the same rate of profits will prevail in the manufacturing sector.

In his correspondence with Ricardo, Malthus criticises the so-called 'corn model', arguing that in no sector of the economy do product and means of production consist of one and the same commodity. Ricardo tackles this objection in *The Principles of Political Economy and Taxation* (1817), resorting to the labour-embodied theory of value (according to which the value of every commodity is given by the quantity of labour directly or indirectly necessary for its production) to measure the surplus and capital advanced. The rate of profits is thus obtained, once again, as the ratio between physically homogeneous quantities (now of labour rather than corn). Taking this line, the theory of value plays a role instrumental to the theory of distribution, which is thus able to bring to the fore the clash of interests between the social classes of workers, capitalists and land-owners.

However, the real importance of Ricardo's theory lies in offering analytic representation – albeit imperfect – of the classical conception of the economic system as a circular flow of production and consumption in a society based on the division of labour. In such a system the product of each firm does not correspond to its requirements in terms of means of production (including means of subsistence for the workers employed); thus, in isolation, no producer is able to continue, but must enter into relations with other sectors of the economy to obtain the necessary means of production in exchange for at least a part of his own product. Thus we have a logical circuit of production and exchange stages, the network that links up the various firms and various sectors of the economy operating in such a way that the economic system continues to function. This is done by guaranteeing each sector the necessary reconstitution of means of production and subsistence, as well as a profit sufficient to induce the firms to go ahead with their activities. As we have seen, the profits, together with the rents (and, possibly, with wages exceeding subsistence level) constitute the result of distribution of the surplus (or, in other words, of what is left of the society's product after all that is needed to reconstitute the means of production and subsistence utilised has been subtracted).

The size of the surplus (Smith's 'wealth of nations' problem), its distribution among the various social classes (the central problem in political economy for Ricardo in his

Principles) and its utilisation in unproductive consumption and accumulation constitute the issues upon which the classical economists focused their attention. The characteristic features of classical political economy are thus division of labour, surplus and the circular production–consumption flow, 'in striking contrast', as Sraffa (1960: 93) pointed out, 'with the view presented by modern theory, of a one-way avenue that leads from "Factors of production" to "Consumption goods"'.

Production of Commodities by Means of Commodities

The analytic representation Ricardo offered of the classical conception of the economy had one particularly important weak point, namely the hypothesis of relative prices proportional to the quantity of labour required for the production of the various commodities, which is inconsistent with the assumption of a uniform rate of profits in the various industries. In *Production of Commodities by Means of Commodities* Sraffa comes up with a solution to the problem framed in terms of the classical conception.

There is therefore a close link between the critical edition of Ricardo's *Works and Correspondence* and the theoretical research Sraffa was himself engaged on. In the 1930s and 1940s work proceeded along two parallel paths; in the latter half of the 1950s, once the work on Ricardo was completed (apart from the volume of indexes, which was to appear only in 1973), Sraffa concentrated on preparing for publication his more strictly analytic contribution, which came out almost simultaneously in English and Italian in 1960.[31]

In Sraffa's analysis, as in that of the classical economists and Marx, the analytic condition upon which determination of the prices of production (the 'natural' prices of the classical economists) rests consists quite simply in an equal rate of profits in the various sectors. This assumption corresponds to the idea pondered by Smith and Marx among others, that the unity of the capitalist system is guaranteed by the free flow of capital from one sector to another in pursuit of the most advantageous utilisation. Nothing, however, is stated on the relations between demand and supply for each commodity; the hypothesis that equilibrium prices correspond to equality between demand and supply, characteristic of marginalist economic theory, finds no place in Sraffa's treatment (a point we shall return to in the following chapter).

Let us now consider the line of investigation followed in *Production of Commodities by Means of Commodities*.

When commodities are at one and the same time products and means of production, the price of one commodity cannot be determined independently of the others, nor the complex of relative prices independently of the distribution of income between profits and wages (which are expressed in terms of the commodity chosen as the unit of measurement, and are thus real wages). One must therefore consider the system as a whole, with all the interrelations running between the various productive sectors, tackling simultaneously income distribution and determination of relative prices.

As a first step, Sraffa (1960: 3) shows that in a system of production for mere subsistence 'which produces just enough to maintain itself', and where 'commodities are produced by separate industries and are exchanged for one another at the market held after the harvest' (i.e. at the end of the production period), 'there is a unique set of exchange values which if adopted by the market restores the original distribution of the products and makes it possible for the process to be repeated; such values spring directly from the methods of production'.

If the economic system under consideration is able to produce a surplus, also 'the distribution of the surplus must be determined through the same mechanism and at the same time as are the prices of commodities'. (Sraffa, 1960: 6) If the wage can exceed subsistence level, the relative prices and one or other of the two distributive variables – wage or rate of profit – are jointly determined, once the technology and the other distributive variable are known; the higher the wage, the lower will be the rate of profits.[32]

Sraffa (1960: 12–13) then goes on to analyse 'the key to the movement of relative prices consequent upon a change in the wage'. As the classical economists and Marx already knew, it 'lies in the inequality of the proportions in which labour and means of production are employed in the various industries'. Indeed, 'if the proportion were the same in all industries no price-changes could ensue', while 'it is impossible for prices to remain unchanged when there is inequality of "proportions"'.

Sraffa also constructs a particular analytic tool, namely the 'standard commodity', thanks to which he is able to solve (part of) the Ricardian problem of an invariable measure of value. Ricardo had in fact attributed two meanings to the notion of a 'standard measure of value', which must not be confused: that of having invariable value (in relation to the complex of the means of production necessary to obtain it) when changes occur in the distribution of income between wages and profits, the technology remaining unaltered; and that of having invariable value in relation to the changes the technology goes through in the course of time (cultivation of ever less fertile lands on the one hand, and technological progress on the other). Having made the distinction between the two problems clear in his 'Introduction' to Ricardo's *Principles* (Sraffa, 1951: xl–xlvii), in *Production of Commodities by Means of Commodities* Sraffa goes on to show how the former can only be solved in terms of a particular analytic construction, the 'standard commodity'. This is a composite commodity (i.e. a set of commodities taken in particular proportions) so determined that the aggregate means of production also correspond to a certain quantity of standard commodity. Thus, with the standard system (and under the assumption that subsistence wages are included in the costs of production) it is possible to determine the rate of profit, just as with Ricardo's 'corn model', as a ratio between two physically homogeneous quantities: the surplus, i.e. the quantity of standard commodity given by the difference between product and means of production, and the means of production advanced by the capitalists. Coming to the second problem – namely invariance in the face of changes in technology – measurement in terms of labour embodied clearly retains significance as a broad indicator of the 'difficulty of production', but there is also an evident risk of bringing metaphysical or subjectivist nuances into play within the economic field (labour as 'toil and trouble').

Nevertheless, with the distinction he draws between the two problems Sraffa offers a precise indication of the limits circumscribing any analytical solution to the question of the standard measure of value, and by so doing he implicitly points up the impossibility of establishing a scientific basis for metaphysical notions of 'absolute value' – a line along which the Torinese economist might have hoped to prompt a reinterpretation of Marx.

Sraffa's analysis of production prices is completed with the case of joint products and, within this category, fixed capital goods and scarce or non-reproducible means such as land. The book closes with a chapter on the choice between economically alternative methods of production in relation to variations in the rate of profits, and with four appendices including the 'References to the literature', where Sraffa explicitly associates himself with the classical economists.

Critique of the marginalist approach

While advancing a theory of production prices within the framework of the classical conception of the functioning of an economic system, Sraffa's book also offers the tools for a radical critique of the marginalist theory of value, aiming at its very foundations. In this respect we can concentrate on two chapters: one on the average period of production, and the final chapter on the choice of techniques.

The concept of the average period of production was used in marginalist theory, and in particular by an exponent of the Austrian school, Böhm-Bawerk (1889), as a measure of the capital intensity of production, interpreting capital as 'waiting time'. Sraffa shows that, depending as it does on the rate of profits, the average period of production cannot be used to measure the quantity of the factor of production capital in the ambit of an explanation of the rate of profits taken as the price of this factor.[33] The difficulty had already been sensed by Wicksell (1934), but modern exponents of the Austrian school, including Hayek (1931a), were later to return to the notion of the average period of production. Harrod, too, in a review of *Production of Commodities by Means of Commodities* (Harrod, 1961), persisted in defending the Austrian theory of value, but Sraffa's brief reply (Sraffa, 1962) suffices to clear up the point once and for all (see Chapter 3).

With regard to the problem of the choice between alternative techniques of production when the rate of profits changes, Sraffa (1960: 103–6) points out the possibility of a 'reswitching of techniques'; in other words, a given technique that proves the most advantageous for a given rate of profits may be superseded by another technique when we raise the rate of profits, but may once again be preferable when the rate of profits rises still higher. The implication here is that however the capital intensity of the two techniques (or in other words the ratio between the quantities utilised of the two 'factors of production', capital and labour) is measured, the general rule that the marginalist theory of value rests on remains contradicted. In fact, the rule takes the distributive values, wage and rate of profits, as prices of the corresponding factors of production determined by the 'law' of demand and supply, so that the quantity of capital should diminish (and the quantity of labour increase) as the rate of profits rises (and the wage consequently falls). With the 'reswitching of technique' Sraffa demonstrates that if this happens when one technique gives way to another with a rising rate of profits, the contrary occurs when the second technology is once again replaced by the first as the rate of profits rises yet higher.

A great deal of debate arose over the above critique (for a survey, see Harcourt, 1972), while the crucial question of its relevance has received relatively scant attention. Contrary to the apparent convictions of many, it applies not only to the aggregate production function (a tool which continues to be used, however, in all the various versions of the dominant macroeconomic theory, from the 'real cycle' theories to the overlapping generations models), but also to all those cases in which, while acknowledging the fact that capital is in reality a collection of various, heterogeneous means of production, the attempt is still made to determine the rate of profits as the price of a factor of production, capital, however it be defined (aggregate of value, 'waiting', average period of production). In particular, Sraffa's critique undermines the very foundations of the idea – crucial to marginalist macroeconomic theory – that a competitive labour market in a closed economy would automatically tend towards full employment equilibrium since the decline in real wages which should attend unemployment would prompt an increase in the quantity of labour employed per unit of capital.[34]

The Sraffian revolution

Taking an overall view of Sraffa's work, we can see it as the sum of three parts: the reconstruction of the real nature of the classical approach with his edition of Ricardo's *Works and Correspondence*; the critique of marginalist theory, whether in the Marshallian version (with the papers of 1925, 1926 and 1930) or in Hayek's macroeconomic version (with the 1932 paper), or as proposing a theory of capital as a factor of production (with the book and the reply to Harrod of 1962); finally, an analysis of value and distribution that is both analytically consistent and rooted in the classical conception of the functioning of the economic system.

Thus with his research Sraffa provides us with all the basic pointers necessary to set economic science on the path away from the marginalist tradition and back towards the classical tradition. Reviving the classical approach, he freed it of the misleading interpretations accrued from marginalist readings; he provides a logically self-consistent solution to the problem of exchange values where Ricardo – and Marx after him – had fallen short of the goal, constituting one of the causes that led to the abandonment of the classical framework and the rise of the marginalist approach. Indeed, Sraffa demonstrates that what the marginalist approach offered was only apparently scientific, but in reality was marred by a basic flaw regarding the theory of capital.

There are at least two points in this contribution that merit closer consideration in view of the interpretative controversy they have given rise to; namely the relevance of his critique of the marginalist theory of value, and the relations between the revival of the classical approach and Keynesian theory. Naturally, we can only offer summary treatment of the two points here.

As we have seen, in *Production of Commodities by Means of Commodities* Sraffa refines the tools for a radical, and indeed destructive critique not only of the version of the marginalist theory that uses an aggregate function of production, but also of all the versions in which the distribution of income among the social classes is tackled as a problem of 'equilibrium prices' (rent, wage and rate of profits) of 'factors of production' (land, labour and capital) determined by demand and supply just like all other commodities. It has been argued that this criticism does not apply to the modern theory of general economic equilibrium, which contains no mechanism to ensure a uniform rate of return on all the various capital goods, if valued in terms of their production costs. However, as early as 1925 Sraffa had pointed out that this approach was in its generality utterly sterile. Indeed, it was precisely for this reason that Sraffa had originally concentrated his critical fire on Marshallian theory, whose apparent realism then exerted (and, despite the lack of any good answer to Sraffa, still exerts, especially for the applied economists) a powerful appeal. After the Marshallian theory,

Sraffa went on in the early 1930s to tackle the somewhat more solid Austrian theory of value, developments of which in the macroeconomic field (particularly by Hayek) seemed at the time to offer the major alternative to the Keynesian theory, then entering the arena. Still susceptible to the appeal of Austrian theory in the 1960s and 1970s we find economists like Harrod and Hicks, but the problems raised by Sraffa – both in his 1932 review of Hayek and in certain chapters of the 1960 book – stand in the way of any progress along this path.

Sraffa's criticisms of the concept of capital also amount – at least in principle – to a deadly blow to the foundations of the so-called 'neo-classical synthesis'. Combining Keynes' thesis on the possibility of fighting unemployment by adopting adequate fiscal and monetary policies with the marginalist tradition of simultaneous determination of equilibrium quantities and prices as a method to study any economic problem, this approach has in the last few decades come to constitute the dominant doctrine in textbooks the whole world over. It is only thanks to increasing specialisation in the various fields of economics, often invoked as the inevitable response to otherwise insoluble difficulties, that the theoreticians of general equilibrium are able to construct their models without considering the problem of relations with the real world that economists are supposed to be interpreting, and that the macroeconomists can pretend that their 'one commodity models' constitute an acceptable tool for analysis. For those who believe that the true task facing economists, hard as it may be, is to seek to interpret the world they live in, Sraffa's 'cultural revolution' still marks out a path for research that may not (as yet) have yielded all it was hoped to, but is certainly worth pursuing.

The problem that, perhaps more than any other, has stood in the way of progress along this path is the difficulty in throwing a bridge to the other major line in non-neoclassical research offered by modern theory, which is the line proposed by Keynes and developed by his most direct followers. Issues like the role of uncertainty and expectations in the economy, the influence of the monetary and financial on real phenomena and the possibility for unemployment to persist alongside unused productive capacity appear, at least at first sight, to have nothing to do with the conceptual world of *Production of Commodities by Means of Commodities*. However, contrasting Sraffian 'long period' analysis with Keynesian 'short period' analysis means contradicting both the conceptual foundations of the classical approach as proposed anew by Sraffa, and those of the Keynesian approach. A solution may be sought – as we seek to argue out more fully in the following chapters – in the recognition that we are faced with a diversity of problems and that there are diverse areas of analysis related together not by the – chimerical – requisite of a general model embracing them all, but by the requisite of 'conceptual consistency', less stringent perhaps, but certainly not lacking in scope for the development of theories within the various fields of analysis.

Notes

1 For fuller details of Sraffa's biography at this stage, see Naldi, 1998a. Among other things, Naldi suggests that Sraffa may have collaborated on the report of the Royal Commission of Investigation, and in particular on the parts concerning concrete economic issues, such as the long section dedicated to the Cassa Veneta dei Prestiti. On Einaudi and Sraffa, see also Faucci, 1986.

2 See Roncaglia, 1984; Ginzburg, 1986; Panico, 1988b; De Cecco, 1993; Ciocca and Rinaldi, 1997.

3 Sraffa's visit to Cambridge was preceded by a letter to Keynes by Mary Berenson, wife of the famous art critic and a friend to Keynes as well as to Gaetano Salvemini (1873–1957), the anti-fascist historian, himself a friend of the Sraffa family. Mary Berenson introduced Sraffa as 'a great friend of the Salveminis [...] Professor Salvemini thinks very well of him.' See Roncaglia, 1983, 1984.

4 See Naldi, 1998a, 1998c.

5 The interpretation presented here was proposed in Roncaglia, 1983. See now Fausti, 1998; Naldi, 1998d.

6 See Spriano, 1970: 150; Spriano, 1977: 108–11; Gerratana, 1991: xlvi. On Gramsci's position on the constituent alliance in the early '30s (at the time painfully isolated within the party) see Spriano, 1969: 281–6.

7 See Roncaglia, 1991.

8 Naldi (1998a: 502) refers to a notebook containing notes on Marshallian theory dated April 1923 and conserved among the Sraffa Papers in Cambridge.

9 See Naldi, 1998b.

10 See Bharadwaj, 1989: Chapter 7 and Ridolfi, 1972.

11 There is actually a case in which the economies external to the firm but internal to the industry prove important, namely that of the industrial districts. See Becattini, 1989. However, this case can obviously not be extended to the *entire* economy, as would be necessary if we were to accept Marshallian theory as a general theory of value for competitive markets.

12 The letter to Keynes in which Sraffa accepts the offer is published in Roncaglia, 1978: 11–13. Together with the *Lecture Notes* conserved in the Sraffa Papers at Trinity College, Cambridge, it is an essential document for our understanding of the development of Sraffa's thinking from 1925 to 1930. See the interpretation presented in Roncaglia 1978, Chapter 1, and in Roncaglia, 1991. Naldi (1998a: 503–4) refers to a note on imperfect competition that Sraffa apparently showed to Maurice Dobb in the spring of 1925 and which, not having used it for the 1925 article, he subsequently returned to on his friend's suggestion when preparing the 1926 article.

13 Not so very curiously, however: little as it may appeal to supporters of the optimality of market economies, the theory of imperfect competition developed following on Sraffa's contribution remains part of the marginalist approach, based as it is on the notion of simultaneous equilibrium of quantity and price determined by the contrasting forces of demand and supply.

14 The crucial point in the development of Sraffa's thinking consists – as he himself points out in the Preface to his 1960 book, and as we shall see more clearly in the following chapter – in the transition from the idea that analysis of competition requires the assumption of constant returns to the idea that no hypotheses on returns need be involved. This transition took place between 1927 and 1930 (probably closer to the latter part of the period), constituting the culmination of Sraffa's efforts, beginning with the 1925 article, to supersede the Marshallian approach.

15 Sraffa, 1930: 93.

16 Marshall's notions of the representative firm and the life cycle of firms aim at making industry equilibrium compatible with the presence of out of equilibrium, growing firms. However, as Kaldor (1934: 61) pointed out, while the product of the individual firm need not be constant (i.e. in equilibrium) in order to have constant output for the industry as a whole (which is needed for the analysis

of supply-and-demand equilibrium), the increase in production of younger firms must exactly compensate the decrease in production of decaying firms. With a stationary age distribution of firms, this requires that each individual firm produces its equilibrium quantity, i.e. the quantity appropriate to the ruling price and cost conditions, and to its age: otherwise, a constant industry output can only be obtained by mere chance. But Marshall does not provide any mechanism ensuring that each individual firm produces the appropriate quantity: the evolutionary conceptual framework is incompatible with the equilibrium method of analysis.

17 See the documentation in the appendix of Naldi, 1998a: 510–12.

18 The letter of resignation, dated 1 November, 1931, is conserved in the Sraffa Papers; the resignation was accepted with decree of 10 November,1931. He was reinstated after the war, together with the few other Italian professors who had not taken the oath of fidelity to fascism, but he remained on leave from his chair in Cagliari up to retirement. In 1953 Sraffa was also elected member of the Accademia Nazionale dei Lincei, where among other things he played a crucial role – together with his friend Sergio Steve – in bestowing the 1966 Francesco Saverio Nitti prize to Ernesto Rossi, one of the founders of the Italian Radical Party, who had studied economics (particularly Wicksteed) in the long years spent in the fascist prisons (Fiori, 1997: 288–90).

19 von Wright, 1958: 15–16.

20 We shall be returning to the subject in Chapter 2.

21 Malcolm, 1958: 69.

22 According to Malcolm (1958: 69), the object of the discussion was Wittgenstein's idea 'that a proposition and that which it describes must have the same "logical form", the same "logical multiplicity"'; according to von Wright, as Malcolm reports in a footnote, the object of the discussion was the idea that each proposition should have a 'grammar'. In a conversation (21 December, 1973) Sraffa confirmed the anecdote, telling me that von Wright was right.

23 Wittgenstein, 1953: 21, 33.

24 See Ranchetti, 1998 for the first attempt to use the Sraffa Papers conserved at Trinity College, Cambridge, to this end.

25 A few months before the *Treatise on Money* had been reviewed by Hayek (1931b), who received a sharp reply from Keynes (1931). On the debate between Hayek and Keynes, see also the other writings contained in Hayek, 1995.

26 Significantly, it is precisely for this reason that a dim view is taken of these debates by a Keynesian of conservative bent like Roy Harrod (1900–78), who rejoiced when Keynes and Hayek subsequently drew closer together: see Harrod, 1951. At the analytic level, the Keynes of the *General Theory* was to adopt a framework differing

at least in part, the Kahnian marginalism of short period equilibrium, which can however be seen above all as a handy sort of scaffolding: see Tonveronachi, 1983.

27 On Dobb's role in the edition of Ricardo's *Works and Correspondence*, see Pollitt, 1988.

28 Letter by Robertson of 3 February, 1935, in Keynes 1973, vol. XIII: 504; and letter by Hicks of 9 April, 1937 in Keynes, 1973, vol. XIV: 81.

29 Schumpeter, 1954: 471.

30 This is the so-called Ricardian theory of rent, or theory of differential rent, which Ricardo actually took from Robert Malthus (1766–1834), and possibly Edward West (1782–1828), while Robert Torrens (1780–1864) advanced it at the same time: in fact, the pamphlets by the four economists came out in rapid succession between 3 and 24 February 1815; see Sraffa's editorial notes in Ricardo 1951, vol. IV: 4–6.

31 The Italian edition was prepared, as hinted at above, at the urge of Sraffa's life-long friend, the prince of Italian bankers, Raffaele Mattioli. The publisher, Giulio Einaudi, was also a friend of Sraffa and the son of his professor, Luigi Einaudi; for years Sraffa was a most respected adviser of his publisher, who played an important role in the shaping of Italian left-wing culture.

32 Let us recall here Sraffa's equations for this case (Sraffa, 1960: 11):

$$(A_a\, p_a + B_a\, p_b + \ldots + K_a\, p_k)(1+r) + L_a\, w = A\, p_a$$
$$(A_b\, p_a + B_b\, p_b + \ldots + K_b\, p_k)(1+r) + L_b\, w = B\, p_b$$
$$\ldots \ldots \ldots \ldots \ldots$$
$$(A_k\, p_a + B_k\, p_b + \ldots + K_k\, p_k)(1+r) + L_k\, w = K\, p_k$$

where $A_a, B_a, \ldots, K_a$; $A_b, B_b, \ldots, K_b$; $\ldots$; $A_k, B_k, \ldots, K_k$ and $L_a, L_b, \ldots L_k$ are the quantities of the various commodities and of labour required for the production of quantities $A, B, \ldots, K$ of the same k commodities; $p_a, p_b, \ldots, p_k$ are the prices of the k commodities; w is the wage rate and r is the rate of profits. We thus have k equations for a system with k commodities, and $k+2$ unknowns (k prices, the wage rate and the rate of profits). Let us choose one commodity as a standard of measure (so that we remain with $k-1$ relative prices as unknowns), and let us consider as exogenously determined either the rate of profits or the wage rate (which is now a real wage rate, being expressed in terms of the commodity chosen as standard of measure): the k equations are now sufficient for determining the k remaining unknowns and, under the assumption that the system produces a surplus (namely that for each commodity the total quantity required as means of production in the various sectors is less or equal to the quantity produced, with the strict inequality holding for at least one commodity), it can be proved that the system has economically meaningful (i.e. positive) solutions for the unknowns. It can also be shown that the rate of profits is a decreasing function of the wage rate, varying from a maximum corresponding to a zero wage rate (the case in which all the surplus accrues to profits) down to zero when the wage rate is maximum (and the whole surplus accrues to wages). See Pasinetti, 1977a, Chapter 5, for a wider mathematical treatment of this simple model.

33 On the same lines, see also Garegnani, 1960.

34 See Roncaglia and Tonveronachi, 1985.

Production of Commodities by Means of Commodities

Between criticism of the marginalist approach and reconstruction of the classical approach

Introduction

Nearly forty years have passed since *Production of Commodities by Means of Commodities* was first published, but interpretation of the text still rouses lively debate. Of course, any particularly concise dissertation – and Sraffa's certainly is that – may be open to various interpretations, but the extraordinary precision of Sraffa's prose should leave little room for misunderstandings to arise. What they arise from, however, is an additional difficulty, namely the radical difference between his type of analysis and the lines of argument customarily followed by the vast majority of the economists of today.

Sraffa himself refers to the problem in the opening lines of his book:

> 'Anyone accustomed to think in terms of the equilibrium of demand and supply may be inclined, on reading these pages, to suppose that the argument rests on a tacit assumption of constant returns in all industries.
>
> (Sraffa, 1960: v)

Two, related, themes emerge from this short passage (and, of course, from the pages that follow it). In the first place, Sraffa suggests that at least two categories of economists exist: those who are 'accustomed to think in terms of the equilibrium of demand and supply', and those who are not.

Secondly, Sraffa points out that a crucial difference between these two groups of economists – or between these two approaches, paradigms or theoretical frameworks – lies in the role played by the quantities produced in analysis of prices and their relationship to income distribution.

This chapter begins by underlining a philologically irrefutable fact: in his analysis Sraffa takes the quantities produced in the various industries as given. As we will see, the reason for this crucial analytical choice lies in the fact that Sraffa isolates a problem – the one concerning the relationship between relative prices and income distribution – and in dealing with it assumes technology as a datum, indeed as the fundamental datum for analysing the issue under consideration. In the absence of assumptions on returns to scale – more specifically, if constant returns to scale are not to be assumed – this implies assuming the quantities produced in the different sectors of the economy as data of the analysis.

This raises a number of questions, particularly in relation to the role played by demand in price determination. We may get these aspects into clearer perspective by reconsidering the distinction between Sraffa's approach and the approach dominating contemporary theory in relation to the analytic structure and 'vision' of the economic process. We then go on to address – again in brief outline – the problem of the differences between the marginalist and the Sraffian approach at the level of method, recalling the influence Sraffa exerted over Wittgenstein. We shall also take a look at the relationship between Sraffa's and Keynes' analyses that we may derive from our interpretation. Finally, the last section summarises the argument developed in this chapter.

The quantities produced assumption

In his analysis Sraffa is quite unequivocal that he takes the quantities produced as given. In a text of exemplary concision, he actually repeats himself to stress the point:

No changes in output and (at any rate in Parts I and II) no changes in the proportions in which different means of production are used by an industry are considered, so that no question arises as to the variation or constancy of returns. The investigation is concerned exclusively with such properties of an economic system as do not depend on changes in the scale of production or in the proportions of 'factors'.

(Sraffa, 1960: v)

For Sraffa the point is not only crucial, but also a potential source of misunderstanding. It is, indeed, an assertion that can hardly go down well with readers taking demand and supply equilibrium theory to their perusal of the book. For such readers – the overwhelming majority of contemporary economists – it is easier to see *Production of Commodities by Means of Commodities* as half (the half they consider the supply side) of a system of general economic equilibrium. Indeed, flying in the face of these explicit statements (which, moreover, are not *obiter dicta* but the pondered opening to a deeply pondered text), a number of economists have advanced this interpretation.[1]

Close on a century after the event, this interpretative error re-evokes the error Marshall made in relation to the theory of Ricardo, and of the classical economists in general. Marshall, as we well know, held that they were aware of only one of the two blades of the scissors determining price – the supply side, but not the demand side.[2] In this case, too, classical analysis was rendered comparable to the analysis in terms of demand and supply equilibrium by introducing the assumption of constant returns. Such an assumption, however, cannot be held to represent a general constitutive element of classical analysis: classical economists had quite different ideas on returns to scale, and moreover conceived them in the context of a dynamic analysis. Let us recall, for example, Smith's ideas about the relationship connecting division of labour (and hence productivity) to the size of the market, or the role played by decreasing returns in agriculture in the analyses of Malthus, West, Torrens, Ricardo and a host of others.

Sraffa, who in his critical edition of Ricardo's *Works and Correspondence* had, among other things, also disputed Marshall's interpretation, foresaw quite clearly that the same error would once again crop up in connection with his own analysis. Indeed, he appeared ready to accept the inevitable, though up to a point. If you really cannot help reasoning in terms of demand and supply equilibrium, he says in effect, then go on and assume – but only as an initial step – that I am considering the case of constant returns:

> If such a supposition is found helpful, there is no harm in the reader's adopting it as a temporary working hypothesis. In fact, however, no such assumption is made.
>
> (Sraffa, 1960: v; these lines come between the first and second of the two passages quoted above)

A problem arises here. If the hypothesis of constant returns constitutes such a dangerous misunderstanding, how can Sraffa possibly deem it acceptable for the first few steps?

Luckily, the answer here is simple enough. The fact is that Sraffa's aim in writing *Production of Commodities by Means of Commodities* was two-fold. On the one hand, he set out to provide the 'prelude to a critique of economic theory', as indicated by the subtitle (where 'economic theory' means 'the marginal theory of value and distribution', as Sraffa himself takes care to specify in his Preface: Sraffa, 1960: vi); at the same time, on the other hand, he intended to solve certain analytical problems – in particular the link between relative prices and distribution of income – that the classical economists had left unsolved, and which had contributed to the crisis of the classical approach and thus the dominance of the marginalist approach. Now, those brought up in the marginalist tradition must first of all learn to recognise the logical difficulties inherent therein; only then will it prove useful to discover that the classical approach is rather more solid than is generally granted, and so discover that it does not collapse simply because the labour theory of value does not hold. But criticisms – or the premises for a critique – of the marginalist theory of value and distribution can perfectly well be advanced, studied and discussed referring to one particular case of marginalist theory itself, namely that of constant returns, considering Sraffa's analysis as 'internal' to the theory of general economic equilibrium *solely to this end*.[3] One point that must be quite clear here, however, is that when we go on from criticism of marginalist theory to reconstruction of the classical approach, the hypothesis of constant returns must be abandoned: as Sraffa repeated, 'no changes in output ... are considered' or, in other words, the quantities produced by the various industries are given.

The clash between the classical and marginalist approaches

Thus, at one and the same time *Production of Commodities by Means of Commodities* constitutes a critique from within the marginalist approach and a contribution within the classical approach. This is possible because certain logical relations must hold in any case; however, they occur in different contexts, as attested by the fact that the hypothesis of constant returns is necessary if we are to read these propositions in the context of marginalist theory, while it is not if we read them as part of classical theory.

The point will emerge more clearly if we turn our attention to the basic differences between the classical and marginalist approaches, considering them as two 'paradigms' (in the sense suggested by Kuhn, 1962) expressing two different conceptions of the way the economic system works. It is a difference that Sraffa points out in the conclusion of his book, in Appendix D, 'References to the literature'. Here Sraffa contrasts 'the picture of the system of production and consumption as a circular process', characterising the classical approach, 'to the view presented by modern theory, of a one-way avenue that leads from "Factors of production" to "Consumption goods"' (Sraffa, 1960: 121).

These expressions sum up radical differences in the 'vision' of the economic world, both in the conceptual apparatus used to represent it and the theoretical structures constructed on those bases.

Let us begin with the classical approach. The economic system is organised on the basis of the division of labour, which does not derive from differences in the original endowment of resources but rather from the intrinsically social nature of men and women.[4] The division of labour is both 'macroeconomic', between sectors, and 'microeconomic', within each production process.[5] As a result of the macroeconomic division of labour, each economic subject – whether individual or firm – must at the end of the production process enter into relationships of exchange with other economic subjects to procure the wherewithal to survive and relaunch the production process. In the economic system as a whole, the quantity of each commodity produced is usually more than enough for these purposes.[6] The portion of the total output which exceeds the strict needs of reproduction – the surplus – may be channelled into consumption exceeding subsistence, or into investments, the choice here being associated with the way in which the surplus is distributed between the various economic subjects.[7] Thus exchange relations are called 'natural' when they express the conditions of reproduction in the circular process of production and consumption, or in other words when each economic subject recovers what is needed to repeat activities in the following period, and when they find it advantageous to do so, since the distribution of surplus respects the condition of uniform rates of profits in the various sectors and thus reflects the essential element of capitalist competition, i.e. the free flow of capital between the various sectors of the economy.[8]

In this tradition the concept of market does not correspond to a point in time and space upon which purchasers and sellers converge, but rather to a network of repetitive and sufficiently regular trade flows, and thus to a network of interpersonal relationships underlying these flows, essential for the reproduction of the economic system. This conception can be found in all the classical economists, at least from William Petty onward.[9] Here prices indicate the conditions for reproduction recalled above, and not the relative scarcity of commodities *vis-à-vis* the wants of consumers.

Thus we find a sharp contrast between the approach of the classical economists and an even older conception, where the concept of market refers to a place in time and space upon which purchasers and sellers converge, and where trade relations are therefore determined by confrontation between demand and supply. The ideal reference point here is the Medieval fair, and then the Stock Exchange. It is from a development of this representation of the economic problem – as determination of the equilibrium arising from the demand/supply confrontation – that the subjective conception of value derives. The 'equilibrium' price (a term that found its place in economics alongside adoption of a methodological model inspired by physics, and in particular static mechanics) is that which ensures equality between demand and supply, or in other words allows for the balancing of opposed forces deriving from the scarcity of commodities and the desire for them. The problem remains essentially the same if it is the original factors of production that are scarce, equilibrium between demand for final consumption goods and the supply of original factors being mediated by production.[10]

In the classical approach, the theory of value is based on technology and the principle for distribution of the surplus – uniform wage rate and uniform rate of profits – taken as given, while the marginalist approach takes as given the endowment of resources and consumers' preferences (to which technology may be added). Here we come to the point of differentiation signalled by Sraffa; according to the classical approach the 'problem of value' does not consist of determining the equilibrium values for prices and quantities exchanged (and quantities produced, where the model includes production) at the same time. More simply, it consists of determining the exchange ratios that satisfy conditions for reproduction of the economic system. Only when the classical and marginalist economic problems are bundled together does it appear necessary in every case – and thus within the classical approach, too – to determine quantities and prices simultaneously.

In the classical approach, of course, separating the problem of 'reproduction prices' from that of quantities produced and exchanged, does not imply that the problem of determining production levels lies outside the economist's field of work. An economist like Marx, who starts from the aforementioned classical approach, makes a clear distinction between three logical stages: the firms' decisions on the quantities to produce, the consequent theoretical analysis of the link between prices and distribution, and finally the problem of 'realising' on the market through sales the value of the commodities produced.

Furthermore, classical economists traditionally consider as separate problems that of determining exchange values (or natural prices) and their relationship with income distribution, and that of the market mechanisms set in action by a discrepancy between supply and demand. These latter mechanisms essentially concern the analysis of competitive processes and, in so far as they do not presuppose a systematic market clearing, do not lead to definite results: 'market prices' are not a theoretical variable explained by a – purely metaphysical – 'principle of gravitation'.[11] Let us stress that all this does not imply that 'demand' – whatever is meant by such a term – has no effect on prices or on produced quantities, within the framework developed by classical economists. 'Demand' influences the entrepreneurs' decisions on how much to produce of each commodity and hence, whenever constant returns do not prevail, the relative 'difficulties of production'; thus 'demand' acts on the data of the problem that Sraffa isolates for analysis. What cannot be found in the Classical (and Sraffian) framework is the assumption of an equilibrium set of prices and quantities determined by market clearing processes and by consumers' choices stemming from 'preference maps' defined by (one-to-one and convex) functions connecting the quantities demanded of the different commodities to prices and to the economic agents' resource endowments. In the classical economists' view, the changes in consumption habits that take place over time are generally the effect rather than the cause of changes in technology and in the structure of production; in any case, these aspects are to be kept well distinct from those concerning the competitive processes of adjustment to the 'sudden changes in channels of trade' (as Ricardo calls them in the title of Chapter 19 of the *Principles*).

Thus, classical economists were used to consider separately different analytical areas. In particular, the analytical problem of determining exchange value is kept distinct from the problem of explaining the realisation on the market of the commodities produced, and from the analysis of competitive processes and market prices.

Various logical areas in economic argumentation may be distinguished; indeed, it is useful to break down into different 'theoretical pieces' the complex issue of analysing how the economic system works: as we shall see, this is a methodological line that Sraffa seems to have suggested in his exchanges with Wittgenstein.

Sraffa and Wittgenstein: the problem of method in economics

In his book Sraffa delimits with close rigour the object of his analysis and thus the data necessary to bring it to a conclusion.[12] The first given datum is the technology; in the absence of hypotheses on returns to scale, this means that the technology corresponds to a given vector of production levels of the various industries.[13] Where a surplus occurs, the manner of distribution must be specified: this Sraffa did taking as given one of the two distributive variables – real wage or rate of profits – and taking the competitive principle of a uniform rate of profits as ruling the division of profits between the various sectors. On this basis, without there being any need for reference to demand, let alone for functions linking the quantities of each commodity in demand to their prices (and, in general economic equilibrium models, to the prices of other commodities, including the services of factors of production), Sraffa shows a way to determine production prices and the residual distributive variable, and to analyse the movements of these variables when the exogenous distributive variable changes.

While – as we have seen – there is no need for direct reference to demand, there is an indirect reference implicit in the assumption of given quantities. It is in fact obvious that the quantities to produce are determined by the decisions of the entrepreneurs, who take into account the foreseeable capacities of market absorption. However, what needs stressing here is that these are *ex ante* entrepreneurial assessments, and not *ex post* findings on consumers' demand; moreover, such assessments are not necessarily point estimates but, as often occurs in reality, may refer to discrete intervals. In practice, what is ruled out is any reference to a demand–supply mechanism for the determination of prices: demand may have a significant but indirect effect on 'natural' prices since, over a period of time, it affects entrepreneurs' decisions concerning productive capacity and the normal degree of plant utilisation, and thus the technology and the relative bargaining power of wage-earners and profit-earners.[14]

This procedure – i.e. rigorous delimitation of the problem, reduced to the interplay of relationships between a limited number of variables – stands in contrast to the approach dominant in modern economic theory.[15] Within the framework of general economic equilibrium all the economic variables – prices, quantities, distributive variables (considered as prices of factor of production services) – are determined at one and the same time in one great analytic scheme. From this standpoint, the criticisms Sraffa raised against the Marshallian theory of the firm (contradiction between the hypothesis of competition and the *ceteris paribus* hypothesis typical of partial equilibria) are sometimes said to hold in relation to partial equilibrium analysis, but to be irrelevant in relation to 'truly general' analysis, which is the only analysis acceptable for the pure theoretician.[16] An analogous evaluation is put forward concerning the 'Cambridge' criticism of the aggregate concept of capital, seen merely as a simplified parabola, a 'low level theory' compared with the 'true' theory, which is general equilibrium.[17]

In every field of science the idea that a general, all-embracing theory is superior to 'partial' theories has shown its appeal. The problem here – at least as far as the marginalist approach is concerned – is whether we are to sacrifice to the fetish of a general theory, either rigour (in the case of the 'parables') or relevance (since the theory of general equilibrium offers scant heuristic scope, once the multiplicity and possible instability of equilibria are granted, and has little to do with the real world once we have recognised the need for hypotheses on the convexity of production and consumption sets, corresponding to the hypothesis of generalised decreasing returns for production and consumption alike). This is no new problem. It has been addressed on various occasions in the philosophical and epistemological debate, and it is worth recalling that, thanks to his influence on Wittgenstein, Sraffa played a leading role here.

Let us briefly recall what has already been discussed in the previous chapter,[18] connecting Wittgenstein's change of views to a comparison between the methodology of general economic equilibrium analysis and the methodology of the 'distinct and separate pieces of analysis' that in our interpretation underlies Sraffa's approach. Originally (in the *Tractatus Logico-Philosophicus* of 1922) Wittgenstein argued a correspondence between the 'facts' constituting the world on the one hand, and 'propositions' constituting our image of the world on the other. Thus we can describe the world with a set of propositions, each one describing a 'fact'. Basically, the 'facts' are the atoms the world is composed of, while the set of propositions describing them offers an axiomatic description of the world itself – or rather, if not all the world, all of the world that can be described in a rational form. About anything else, that is, in those cases where no rational description can be supplied, 'one must be silent'.[19]

The marginalist theory of general economic equilibrium seems to be founded on philosophical positions much like those of this early Wittgenstein: an atomist base ('economic subjects' and 'commodities'), correspondence between the facts of the world and the elements of theory, and the claim of a complete description according to general rules of all that is describable in the world (the general theory).

However, Wittgenstein eventually abandoned this conception, and he did so – as he himself notes in his preface to the *Philosophical Investigations* (published posthumously in 1953) – under the influence of long discussions with Sraffa. In particular, Wittgenstein abandoned the idea of language as axiomatic representation of the world and the idea of the 'unspeakable'. Instead, he developed the idea of 'language games', namely models that focus the attention on particular aspects of real language, presenting them as the general language of a group of people. One commentator interpreted it thus: 'There is not [...] any unique analysis of propositions into their intrinsically unanalysable elements. What sort of analysis will be useful and provide a real clarification depends on the circumstances, on just what is problematic about the propositions under examination.'[20]

Of course, this is not to say that having criticised the early stages of Wittgenstein's reflections Sraffa then went on to endorse the conclusions. Nevertheless, we can see a distinct analogy with the method Sraffa follows in his book, focusing on a specific problem (fundamental as it may be) and on those variables directly relevant to the problem in question, but without denying the existence of other problems to be addressed with other 'language games' and, in particular, without denying the indirect influence of other variables.

If this point is accepted, it will become perfectly clear how inappropriate are any attempts to extrapolate mechanically, from the analysis illustrated in *Production of Commodities by Means of Commodities*, Sraffa's theoretical position in other fields – for example, ascribing to him a quantity theory of money.[21] In other words, we cannot expect to 'extend' Sraffa's analysis by associating with his equations other equations taken to be in the same 'logical area' or part of the same 'language game'. Nevertheless, this is precisely how neoclassical interpreters act when they set out to complete the half system of general economic equilibrium Sraffa is supposed to have analysed, adding to his 'supply' equations the appropriate demand equations.

A point worth stressing here is that this difference in method holds important implications for the significance to be attached to the concepts Sraffa analyses, generating appreciable differences from the corresponding concepts as approached with marginalist analysis. In particular, within the marginalist approach the concept of equilibrium refers to a state of equality between demand and supply (market clearing) throughout the economy while, within the classical approach, as far as the concept is applicable,[22] reference is simply made to the absence of incentives to transfer capital from one sector of the economy to another ('competitive equilibrium'). Thus it is evidently a mistake to confuse Sraffa's prices of production (and the natural prices of the classics) with the 'normal prices' or 'long period equilibrium prices' in marginalist analysis.

At this point we come up against a problem which we shall very briefly outline here. If we accept the idea of separation between the various 'language games', or in other words between analyses of different problems – for example, if we distinguish the analysis of the prices-distribution link from the analysis of the factors determining levels of production or technology, or the distribution of income itself – there will no longer be any need to verify the possibility of constructing a single general model in which to include the various 'pieces of analysis' as fitting parts of a whole. Actually, each 'piece of analysis' implies a distinct process of abstraction, and thus belongs to its own 'analytic area', and no classification of decreasing generality can be determined between the various areas.[23] There is, however, the problem of the internal consistency of the conceptual framework – or conception of the way the economic system functions – within which the various 'pieces of analysis' addressing the different problems are inserted. For example, a 'monetary' explanation of the rate of profits as referred to by Sraffa (and which we shall be returning to shortly) is not compatible with a marginalist theory of value, where the distributive variables are the prices of the services of productive factors. Another issue we may consider in this light – as a problem of the consistency of the conceptual frameworks in which the two analyses are embedded – is the complex question of the relationship between Sraffa's and Keynes' analyses.[24]

Sraffa and Keynes

Thus, as we have seen, Sraffa's analysis may be located as falling within a classical conception, where the task assigned to economic theory is to establish the conditions for reproduction of the system and to analyse its evolution over time. The various problems are obviously connected, but can be analysed separately. This applies in particular to the quantities produced by the various industries, which Sraffa – as we noted above – takes as an external given for the purposes of his analysis. Here we find a bridge reaching out in the direction of Keynes' analysis of the possibility of persisting situations of under-employment.

The best way to approach this issue is step-by-step, considering in succession the conception within which Sraffa's analysis is inserted, the applicability of 'Say's law' to Sraffa's analysis, the relationship between prices of production and market prices, Sraffa's indirect reference to Keynesian theory and, finally, the 'bridge' that can be built between the two analyses.

As we have seen, although presented in a way that is formally compatible with marginalist analysis (in such a way that criticism of it can be developed from within), Sraffa's analysis was conceived in terms of a classical approach, albeit making a great stride ahead at the level of analytic rigour and with precise delimitation of the problem addressed. The classical approach revolves about the concept of surplus: its production, circulation through trade, distribution among the various social classes and the uses it is put to, i.e. accumulation or consumption beyond the bare necessities. Each of these aspects is related to the others, but for the sake of analysis it is better to take them in isolation: thus, for example, for the theory of production we have Smith's analysis (and Babbage's, and John Stuart Mill's) of the factors determining the division of labour; we then have the theory of value in connection with exchange ratios, and their relationship with distributive variables; analyses carried out by Smith, Ricardo, Marx and various others for the theory of distribution; the classical theory of accumulation, and as a separate issue, what Marx described as the problem of realisation, i.e. sale of the quantities produced, with its logical appendix, the theory of crises. In other words, we have a range of fields of analysis within each of which variables taken as given in other theories are to be accounted for, while variables explained in other 'pieces of analysis' are taken as given. This is, in fact, a procedure that Sraffa follows rigorously, 'cutting out' the problem of determination of technology or quantities produced, which lie 'upstream' from his analysis, but at the same time isolating his problem from what lies 'downstream' like the question of realisation, or the relationship between prices of production and market prices.

Given this practice, there are clearly no grounds to argue that Sraffa adheres to 'Say's law', which states that 'supply creates its own demand'. Quite simply, the problem of realisation is not addressed, and there is therefore no reason why there should be any automatic correspondence between aggregate demand and supply.[25] Actually, there would be no good reasons why one should not argue the contrary, either, were it not for the requisite of consistency with the 'conceptual framework' Sraffa's analysis works in. In fact, in the presence of savings and financial circuits, 'Say's law' (in the interpretation now dominant, as a proposition regarding macroeconomic equilibrium) implies that the rate of interest is determined by the equilibrium between demand and supply of loanable funds, and thus implies the uniqueness of the real equilibrium, also for distribution variables, in contrast with one of the mainstays in Sraffa's analysis.

Another point to clear up in this connection is the distinction between natural prices (or prices of production) and market prices. Sraffa confines discussion to pointing out, quite clearly, that his argument 'contains no reference to market prices' (Sraffa, 1960: 9). This means that there is no textual evidence to ascribe to Sraffa the idea that prices of production are 'centres of gravity' for market prices, let alone attributing to him a conception of market prices as a theoretical variable determined (in some version of Marshallian short period) by the interplay of demand and supply. Bearing in mind that the problem of realisation comes in logical sequence after the problem addressed by Sraffa, together with the fact that there is no good reason to establish any formal connection between prices of production and market prices (of the type of the connection between long and short period to be found in Marshallian theory), there is no reason to assume that the quantities produced coincide with the quantities in demand when prices of production prevail (Smith's 'effectual demand'), commodity by commodity.[26] Obviously, this is a prerequisite for claiming that Sraffa does not adhere to 'Say's law', which in fact concerns this equality in the aggregate. Of course, if the technology is such as is 'socially necessary', and thus corresponds to what entrepreneurs consider a normal utilisation of productive capacity, we must conclude that this equality occurs over the average of a number of periods if the entre-preneurs' expectations are to be satisfied. However, in the course of time productive capacity changes (in general, grows). Consequently the realisation on the average, over a span of several years, of a normal degree of utilisation of productive capacity, holds no implications for any of the periods taken individually regarding the relationship between quantities taken as given (which may differ from those effectively produced if the degree of effective utilisation differs from what entrepreneurs see as normal) and quantities in demand at the natural price.

We may, moreover, wonder what possible reason there could be, if not respect for the marginalist (or, more generally speaking, subjectivist) tradition, for adding the condition of equality between demand and supply to that of uniformity of the rate of profits in the various sectors of the economy invoked by the classicists in their theory of competition. Indeed, we might say that, with his clear distinction between the various problems, Sraffa achieved a far greater clarity than those classical economists who had sought a compro-mise with the subjectivist tradition.[27]

In the light of all these points we can begin to see some connection between Sraffa's analysis and Keynes'. Of course, the two analyses refer to different problems, and therefore cannot come into direct logical contradiction with each other. Moreover, if we avoid the neoclassical interpretations of Keynes (disregarding the question as to how much Keynes might have laid himself open to them), the two analyses refer to a largely shared conceptual framework, so that 'indirect' contradictions are avoided as well. In particular, both analyses reject the prices–quantities equilibrium associ-ated with the full employment of resources: Sraffa with his criticism of the marginalist theory of capital and distribu-tion, Keynes with his opposition to the orthodox theory of interest.

Sraffa, for his part, appears to consider his analysis open to integration with central aspects of the Keynesian framework – though not necessarily with Keynes's specific theories. We may interpret in this direction an often-quoted passage of Sraffa's book:

> The rate of profits [...] is [...] susceptible of being determined from outside the system of production, in particular by the level of the money rates of interest.
>
> (Sraffa, 1960: 33)

A dominant theme of Keynesian theory is that monetary and financial variables play a crucial role in determining the real variables (level of investments, income, employment).[28] In the passage cited above Sraffa seems to be opening the way for a similar thesis on the distribution of income: contractual wage bargaining between entrepreneurs and unions determines the monetary wage, but the level of the real wage will depend upon money prices, which in turn depend on manifold elements including production and employment, but also the liquidity of the system and currency exchange rates.[29] The similarity between the two theses, and the fact that Sraffa did not intend to address the problem of distribution in depth with these observations, suggest that one of Sraffa's concerns here, if not his primary concern, may have been to underline the similarity between his outlook and Keynes'. Furthermore, in the Preface to *Production of Commodities by Means of Commodities* Keynes is mentioned with reference to the assumption of given quantities (see Chapter 1, this edition).

The 'bridge' between Sraffa's analysis of prices and Keynes' analysis of production levels can be built along the following lines. In Sraffa's analysis, which looks to conditions for reproduction of the economic system, the prices of commodities used as means of production are equal to the prices of the same commodities included in the product, and the technology is given. When the technology changes, if we rule out the entirely hypothetical case of a proportional reduction in all the coefficients of production, the relative prices also change. If the changes in technology were known *ex ante*, we would have continual arbitrage between current and future production, with a mechanism of forward prices and own interest rates which, significantly, constitutes a theoretical contribution by Sraffa (1932) taken up (and reworked, introducing expectations) by Keynes in the crucial Chapter 17 of his *General Theory*.[30] In general, however, it is impossible to take changes in technology as known *ex ante* (particularly when referring not to productivity growth in the economy or in the manufacturing sector as a whole, but to sectoral technical changes, as is necessarily the case in the context of an analysis of relative prices). Indeed, we may argue that it is precisely here that there arises the major element – in so far as it operates continually and systematically, even in 'normal times' – of that all-pervasive uncertainty constituting a key feature of Keynes' vision, leading him to grant expectations a central role in his theory. For this reason the two problems – Sraffa's and Keynes' – must be kept apart. Nevertheless, given Sraffa's approach to his problem – isolating it from the problem of determination of quantities produced while avoiding any opening in the direction of 'Say's law' – we may consider his analysis of the prices–distribution link conceptually compatible with Keynes' analysis of employment, once the latter has been cleared of marginalist encrustations.

Summing up

In synthesis, *Production of Commodities by Means of Commodities* may be the object of two quite different readings. On the one hand, we may draw from Sraffa's book a number of analytical results that can be used for a critique from within demolishing the traditional marginalist theories of value and distribution; in this context, other parts of the book – such as the discussion of the 'standard commodity' – may appear pleonastic or esoteric. On the other hand, we may read Sraffa's book as a decisive contribution for an analytically solid reconstruction of the classical approach. The distinction between these two different readings is connected to recognition of the existence of two clearly distinct representations of the working of market economies, the classical one based on the circular flow of production and consumption and on the notion of the surplus, and the marginalist one based on the one-way avenue leading from factors of production to consumption goods and the satisfaction of consumers' preferences.

Missing the distinction between these two different readings of Sraffa's book has often led to a number of crucial misunderstandings. Specifically, on the one hand Sraffa's critical contribution has been reduced to a nihilist, purely destructive attitude; on the other hand, the constructive elements of Sraffa's analysis have been overlooked or inserted in an inappropriate framework. Yet, the distinction between the two readings is clearly stated, already in the opening pages, in Sraffa's book. Keeping this into account, as well as the hints we may draw from the Sraffa–Wittgenstein connection, we may appreciate the 'open' nature of Sraffa's constructive contributions, and specifically the possibility of integrating the classical and Keynesian approaches.

Notes

1 See e.g. Johnson, 1962; Robinson, 1961; Hahn, 1982. Joan Robinson did, however, eventually modify this interpretation: see Robinson, 1978: 122.

2 See in particular the appendix to Marshall's *Principles* (1961: 813–21); here we find – on p. 820 – the famous reference to the blades of scissors:

> The 'cost of production principle' and the 'final utility' principle are undoubtedly component parts of the one all-ruling law of supply and demand; each may be compared to one blade of a pair of scissors. When one blade is held still, and the cutting is effected by moving the other, we may say with careless brevity that the cutting is done by the second; but the statement is not one to be made formally, and defended deliberately.

3 In this connection it is worth pointing out that Sraffa himself refers to part III of his book, dedicated to the 'switch in methods of production', as an exception with regard to the absence of any

hypothesis on returns. Here we must, in fact, consider changes – albeit only notional – 'in the proportions in which different means of production are used by an industry' (Sraffa, 1960: v). However, essential as it is for criticism of the traditional marginalist theory of value and distribution, this part is of minor utility for understanding the phenomena of technological change. To this end it is more useful to adopt a dynamic evolutionary approach, as did the classical economists from Smith's theory of the development of the division of labour to Babbage's 1832 theory of the links between division of labour and mechanisation. See Corsi, 1991.

4 Smith, who insisted on this point in the *Wealth of Nations*, came in for severe criticism from Pownall, 1776: see Roncaglia, 1995a. According to the marginalist conception (and Pownall might be considered a precursor of it from this viewpoint), by contrast, the division of labour arises from differences in the abilities of the various workers.

5 Analysis of the division of labour can be carried out from various viewpoints. For example, the distinction between the horizontal and vertical division of labour is relevant to analysis of the link between technological change and evolution in the social structure. Moreover, the microeconomic division of labour (or organisational division of labour) is itself a source of the macroeconomic division of labour: consider the case of certain areas of activity externalised by firms, giving rise to new firms. On these points see Corsi, 1991.

6 Strictly speaking, this applies to a closed economic system. For an economy open to foreign trade, we might see exchange between domestic and foreign commodities as an additional production process, with a procedure much like the 'closure' of input-output tables.

7 Let us remember that product, total means of production and surplus are all vectors. The distribution of the surplus (between social classes and between sectors) occurs in terms of value, and is thus connected to the determination of exchange ratios.

8 The labour theory of value in this respect (disregarding, therefore, its 'metaphysical' aspect, connected to the idea of labour as 'cause' or 'substance' of value) is merely a simple way of expressing the relative difficulty in the production of a commodity using a one-dimensional variable. However, the second condition for reproduction (uniformity of the rate of profits in the various sectors) calls for a multi-dimensional description of the 'difficulty of production': for each sector, a vector including as many elements as there are means of production (including labour) represents the 'physical costs of production'.

9 See Roncaglia, 1985: 73–6.

10   Actually, the very idea of original factors of production needs looking closely. In fact, 'land' normally requires substantial investment before it can be used in the production process, but it cannot be considered scarce in absolute terms. As regards 'labour', we must bear in mind both the importance of professional training in contemporary economies and a whole range of elements (from customary practices and legal norms to the existence of social services such as the provision of kindergartens) determining both rates of activity (especially for women) and migratory flows. After long debate it has been concluded that it is erroneous to consider 'capital' an original factor of production. As for 'entrepreneurial' qualities, their presence (and measurement) are defined *ex post* on the basis of the economic results of the firms; hence they cannot be inserted in production functions representing alternatives between which the producer can choose.

11   See for example Smith, 1976: Book I, Chapter 7 (and the comment in Roncaglia, 1990b), or Ricardo, 1951: Chapters 19 and 30.

12   In a certain sense the exact delimitation of a problem corresponds to its solution. Such is the case, for example, with the Ricardian problem of the invariable standard of value. For Ricardo, the standard of value must be unvarying with respect to changes in both technology and the distribution of income. However, set in these terms, the problem remains insoluble. With his analysis of the 'standard commodity' Sraffa delimits the problem, restricting the focus to changes in distribution and singling out a commodity that does not vary in terms of its means of production, since these are nothing else but a certain quantity of the same commodity. (It is therefore a mistake to say that Sraffa 'solves' the original Ricardian problem of the invariable standard of value.) Cf. Roncaglia, 1978: Chapter 4.

13   Moreover, in the general case where fixed capital goods are present, the technology employed as given for the determination of prices corresponds to what is considered a normal degree of utilisation of plant; it is in fact to this specification of technology that firms make reference for decisions on prices. On this point, and on the concept of 'socially necessary' technique, see Roncaglia, 1978: 27–9; 1995b. It is a point worth stressing; in Sraffa's analysis it is technology that is taken as directly given (such that one may see the technology implicit in the equations as deriving – through a procedure of abstraction – from the technology actually prevalent), while the production levels of the various sectors are taken as 'indirectly' given, being – in the absence of hypotheses on returns to scale – implicit in the technology (so that they do not have as 'direct' empirical correlate the levels of production actually prevailing at a given time).

14 This is the dynamic evolutionary view that, for example, also includes Smith's theorem according to which the division of labour (and thus the technology) is limited by the extent of the market (i.e. by demand, but in the broad sense, and not as a functional relationship linking quantities in demand with prices and incomes).

15 The method Sraffa follows is in some ways closer to the idea of Marshall (and later Keynes) of focusing on 'short causal chains'. This is because each link between cause and effect is an abstraction and as such disregards a great many secondary elements; thus it seems likely that the distortions due to disregarded elements can add up in a long chain of causal links, leaving any connection between the initial and final terms extremely unreliable. We might say that Sraffa's method consists of focusing on one link in the chain. Of course, while in this respect there is some analogy in the method between Marshall and Sraffa, there are wide differences in their conceptions of the way the economy functions; let us recall that Marshall employs the concept of equilibrium between demand and supply, and thus evidently conceives of partial equilibrium analysis (of the firm or the industry) as a segment of general economic equilibrium analysis.

16 See Samuelson, 1987: 458–9; Newman and Vassilakis, 1988. Actually, as already stressed above (Chapter 1: 12ff.), the criticisms launched by Sraffa in the articles of 1925 and 1926 are far more radical, regarding the very foundations of analyses based on functional relationships between cost and quantities produced and the hypothesis on the convexity of production functions. See Roncaglia, 1978: 10 ff., 104 ff.

17 In reality the 'Cambridge' criticisms concerned the aggregate concept of capital only initially (Robinson, 1953), but subsequent to the publication of Sraffa's book (and of Garegnani, 1960) the emphasis shifted to the concept of capital as a 'factor of production' (and, correlatively, to the notion of profit as the price for the service of this factor of production). See Chapter 1: 37ff.

18 For a wider exposition, see Roncaglia, 1978: Chapter 7.

19 '1   The world is everything that is the case. ...
   1.2 The world divides into facts. ...
   3   The logical picture of the facts is the thought. ...
   4   The thought is the significant proposition. ...
   4.26 The specification of all true elementary propositions describes the world completely. ...
   7   Whereof one cannot speak, thereof one must be silent.'
        (Wittgenstein, 1922: 31, 43, 61, 91, 189).

20 Quinton, 1968: 12–13.

21 See Boffito, 1973: 89.

22 As we have seen, in the marginalist tradition the concept of equilibrium derives from physics, and more precisely from classical mechanics, reference to conditions of equilibrium implying static analysis. By contrast, reference to the dichotomy between static and dynamic analysis appears inappropriate in terms of the classical approach; see Roncaglia, 1978: 119.

Some post-Keynesian economists (see e.g. Kaldor, 1972) have argued that the concept of equilibrium is to be rejected *in toto*, given the frequent occurrence of increasing returns in the economy. There are good reasons for this idea, if reference is to the notion of equilibrium imported from classical mechanics into marginalist theory; but there is some exaggeration, if rejection also involves the competitive hypothesis of a uniform rate of profits in the various sectors of the economy, as employed by the classical economists and Sraffa.

23 For example, it would indeed be difficult to attempt such a comparison between Sraffa's analysis of prices and Harrod's analysis of the warranted growth rate. The term 'analytic area' was suggested by Ian Steedman since it does not imply the possibility of ordering in a sequence of decreasing abstraction the different 'analytic areas'. This idea was possibly suggested by the term 'analytic level' that I had been using in previous works (and in previous drafts of the present chapter). The term 'field of analysis' is also better discarded, since it is commonly used for designating sufficiently homogeneous sets of objects of analysis, while here we refer to the technique of analysis, and specifically to the choices made in the process of abstraction underlying any theoretical reasoning.

24 For an attempt along these lines, see Roncaglia, 1995b.

25 Again, a notion that has absolutely nothing to do with classical political economy is that of 'normal long period positions' of the economy employed, for example, by Garegnani, 1988. See Roncaglia, 1990b, where Smith's concept of natural price is discussed.

26 Actually, the problem of the relationship between quantities produced and quantities in demand – the problem of realisation – simply does not arise in Sraffa's 1960 field of analysis.

27 On the 'shifting' of the post-Ricardian classical economists in this direction – attributing to market prices the status of theoretical variable – see Bharadwaj, 1978; the main references are to the late writings of De Quincey and to John Stuart Mill. Smith's 'compromise', on the other hand, consisted in isolating the natural price as a theoretical concept, relegating the role of demand and supply

to influences on the market price, although no theoretical analysis is made of how the latter is determined. See Roncaglia, 1990b. However, as noted in Chapter 2: 53, in the subjective theory of value, demand and supply (scarcity and utility) are the key factors in the price determination mechanism, both for short-run (market) and long-run (normal) prices.

28 On the basis of the Sraffa Papers housed in Trinity College, Cambridge, Ranchetti, 1998 offers new information on Sraffa's attititude to Keynes' theory. In fact, Sraffa's criticisms of Keynes' theory of liquidity preference seem to be looking for a greater degree of radicalism in Keynes's reversal of the traditional marginalist thesis of the 'real' determination of the natural interest rate. Sraffa's criticisms concern both the direction of the causal link (not from the 'quantity of money' to the interest rate but vice-versa, with an endogenous theory of the supply of money much like the one subsequently developed by various post-Keynesians) and the attempt to express the demand for money for speculative purposes as a decreasing function of the interest rate defined in a sufficiently univocal way (although Keynes makes the attempt with far more caution than the 'Keynesian' manuals suggest, given the role he attributes to expectations and their extreme variability). Sraffa also seems to be looking for a greater degree of radicalism when criticising the confusion Keynes ran into between own rates of interest and the marginal efficiency of capital goods in chapter XVII of the *General Theory*.

29 See Roncaglia, 1993 for indication of the lines along which to develop an analysis of income distribution conceptually compatible with Sraffa's prices-distribution link. Alternative suggestions based on the link between interest rate and rate of profits are offered by Panico, 1988 and Pivetti, 1991.

30 On the relationship between Sraffa's 1932 article and the chapter in Keynes, 1936, see Kregel, 1983 and Tonveronachi, 1991. More generally, for interpretations of Keynes oriented in the direction suggested here, see Kregel, 1976 and Tonveronachi, 1983.

Chapter 3

The Sraffian schools

Introduction

This chapter aims to provide a broad overview of the role played in the current economic debate by the contributions by Piero Sraffa and those contemporary economists who share his proposal of a return to the approach of the classical economists, from William Petty to François Quesnay, from Adam Smith to David Ricardo, up to Karl Marx. It must be stressed immediately that our discussion of the different positions will not be neutral, because of the direct participation of the present writer in the debate to be surveyed in the following pages.

The previous chapters have considered the cultural project pursued by Sraffa: to shunt the car of economic science back on the road initiated by the classical approach, which has been submerged for over a century by the marginalist approach. Now we will briefly survey the contributions offered to such a cultural project by a continuously increasing number of economists, since the publication of *Production of Commodities by Means of Commodities* in 1960. For ease of exposition, we have distinguished such contributions into three groups: the critique of various aspects of marginalist theory; the defence and development of the classical conceptual framework reconstructed by Sraffa, in particular with his critical edition of Ricardo's *Works and Correspondence*; the development of Sraffa's (1960) analysis of the relationship between relative prices and income distribution.

The contributions illustrated in these three sections share a common foundation – the critique of the marginalist approach – but they also occasionally display some differences concerning the lines of research along which to develop the reconstruction of political economy suggested by Sraffa. Once again for ease of exposition, we will concentrate attention on three main lines of research, that appear more widely developed at least at the present stage of the debate: respectively, those connected especially with the names of Luigi Pasinetti, Pierangelo Garegnani and Paolo Sylos Labini. More precisely, we will consider in its broad outline the 'Ricardian' proposal of reconstruction of classical political economy as developed mainly in Pasinetti's writings; we will briefly illustrate Garegnani's 'Marxian' proposal and we will turn to Sylos Labini's (and the present writer's) 'Smithian' proposal. A tentative evaluation of the three lines of research is then presented, while the last section provides a brief summary of the chapter.

Two warnings are in order from the outset. First, the reference to Smith, Ricardo and Marx for identifying the three lines of research is simply an expository device, which holds good for some aspects but not for others. Secondly, the differences – which should not be exaggerated – mainly concern the 'bets' on the perspectives of the different lines of research proposed for the reconstruction of economics within a substantially common paradigm, that of the classical approach. Thus the different lines of research should not be crystallised into rival 'schools'. The title of this chapter, which might seem to suggest this idea, aims in fact at countering an opposite misunderstanding, which is more widespread and more dangerous: the idea that there is a monolith, the 'Sraffian school', characterised by complete identity of views on the most disparate economic issues on the part of its adherents. Independently from the specific ideas which will be presented on the greater or smaller potentialities of the three lines of research, the following pages point to the wealth of contributions springing from within the stream of thinking christened in turn, and always reductively, 'Sraffian' or 'neo-Ricardian school'.

The critique of the marginalist theory

As already noted, Sraffa aims at a complete turnaround of economic science, rejecting the dominant marginalist approach and proposing in its place the classical economists' approach. The first step in this direction is his critique of the marginalist approach, which dominated academic teaching both in Italy and in Anglo-Saxon countries (Sraffa, 1925; 1926; 1930). The second step is the critical edition of Ricardo's writings (Ricardo, 1951–55), where the web of concepts and the analytical scheme constituting the foundation of classical political economy are re-proposed, cleared from the misinterpretations superimposed in nearly a century of marginalism. Finally, the third and analytically decisive step arrives with the publication, in 1960, of *Production of Commodities by Means of Commodities*: an analysis of the relationship between relative prices and income distribution that provides, at the same time, the basis for an internal logical critique of traditional marginalist theories of value and distribution, and the solution to certain problems left unsolved by classical theorists, providing more solid ground for the reconstruction of classical political economy.

Traditionally, the marginalist approach conceives the problem of value as concerning the determination of 'equilibrium' prices and quantities, namely such as to ensure the equality between supply and demand, and hence stemming from the confrontation of the initial endowments of productive resources and the preferences of economic agents. (This 'vision' of the economy remains unchanged when from pure exchange models we go on to the models considering both exchange and production, so that the relationship between pure endowments and preferences is mediated by productive activity, side by side with exchange and consumption activities; nor does it change when productive endowments include produced means of production side by side with given productive resources.)

Confronted with the problem of value thus defined, traditional marginalist theories (those theories that Keynes unfortunately called 'classical', pointing as an example to Pigou's analysis) had as their central tenet the thesis that an economic system where perfect competition prevails and which is not subject to repeated exogenous disturbances tends to an equilibrium position that is also an optimum, in the sense that it is not possible to improve the position of any economic agent without worsening the position of some other agent. In particular, traditional marginalist theories maintain that under perfect competition the real wage moves towards a level which ensures the equality between demand and supply of labour, that is full employment. Among the automatic equilibrating mechanisms bringing the economy towards full employment, traditional marginalist theories stressed the flexibility of the capital–labour ratio: if the real wage falls under the pressure of unemployment, firms will find it more profitable to utilise productive techniques employing more workers and less capital, so that the capital–labour ratio falls, and a given endowment of 'capital' is compatible with the employment of an increasing number of workers, up to full employment.

This thesis took different forms in authors belonging to different streams of the marginalist approach. Garegnani (1960) examines the theories developed by a few representative writers within this tradition (Walras, Böhm-Bawerk, Wicksell), bringing out explicitly the criticisms which in Sraffa (1960) are formulated in their most essential terms. In this context we may point out that Sraffa's critique is more general than that developed (on at least partly parallel lines) by Joan Robinson (1953), which directly refers to the aggregate notion of capital, used in the so-called aggregate production function. Sraffa's critique of marginalist theories refers more generally to the very idea that the 'prices' of 'factors of production' (identified with capital and labour) are determined by supply and demand forces, that is, indirectly, by the comparison of resource endowments and consumers' final preferences.

The analytical point on which Sraffa concentrates attention concerns the consequences of the fact that 'capital' is a set of produced means of production, the relative prices of which change in a non-univocal way when income distribution changes, so that it is impossible to state *a priori* whether a real wage reduction provokes an increase in the use of labour relatively to 'capital'. For the analytical details of the debate the reader is referred to, for example, Harcourt (1972); here we only note that Sraffa's critique hits, behind the traditional marginalist theories of distribution, the idea of a self-regulating market, and the conception of economics as the science which concentrates on studying the market's equilibrating mechanisms.

As is well known, Sraffa's book only purports to 'serve as the basis' for a critique of the marginalist tradition. As already noted, simultaneously with Sraffa and following similar lines of enquiry, Garegnani (1960) puts forward a direct critique of some of the main theoretical contributions in the marginalist tradition. The publication of Sraffa's book was followed by a lively debate. A first skirmish (Harrod, 1961; Sraffa, 1962) clarifies that the possibility of measuring capital, once the rate of profits is given, does not constitute a reply to Sraffa's strictures, since these refer to the necessity, for the traditional marginalist theories of distribution, to measure capital *independently* of income distribution between wages and profits (a point which Garegnani 1960 stresses as well). A second clash begins with Samuelson's (1962) attempt to depict the aggregate production function as a 'parable' not betraying the essential characteristics of a productive system; and by Levhari's (1965) attempt to show that the problems raised by Sraffa (such as the possibility of the 'reswitching of techniques') refer only to the single industry, and not to the economic system as a whole. These propositions are immediately refuted.[1] The debate then turns to the issue of the relevance of the Sraffian critiques for the foundations of the marginalist approach; the claim that such critiques only concern the 'lowbrow' versions of the marginalist theories[2] implies a retreat towards the rarefied atmosphere of intertemporal general economic equilibrium models, and the abandonment of the assumption of a rate of profits uniform across the various sectors of the economy.[3]

Sraffa's analysis also provided the foundations for basic criticisms of specific varieties or specific aspects of the marginalist approach.

Among the critiques of specific varieties of the marginalist approach, let us recall those proposed by Steedman of the value and distribution theory as originally proposed by Jevons and by Wicksteed.[4] Pasinetti also criticised Solow's use of the Fisherian notion of the rate of return, which Solow considers as 'the central notion of capital theory', since it is assumed to be an index of the 'quantity of capital' which can be defined independently of the rate of profits, so that it can be used for explaining the latter.[5]

Among the critiques of specific aspects of the marginalist approach, let us recall the critiques of the Heckscher–Ohlin–Samuelson theory of international trade. According to this theory, each country tends to specialise in the production of commodities that require relatively larger quantities of those factors of production which are relatively more abundant in that country. These critiques were originally proposed independently by Parrinello (1970) and by Metcalfe and Steedman (1972, 1973), and were then developed in a long series of articles, sometimes attempting as well to build a 'neo-Ricardian' theory of international trade.[6]

Also, some commonplaces in marginalist theory were criticised by Steedman, referring to the theories of consumers' choices, technical progress, and fiscal incidence.[7] We have then to recall the critiques of the 'neoclassical synthesis', specifically of Modigliani's (1944, 1963) attempt to set up a theory of income and employment retaining the basic principles of the marginalist tradition, while opening the door to the use of fiscal and monetary Keynesian policies.[8] Another aspect of the 'neoclassical synthesis', and more generally of mainstream macroeconomic theory – namely the assumption of a 'representative agent', a trick that can be considered the other face of the choice of single-commodity models – has been criticised in various works by Lippi and others.[9]

As we can see, the critique of the marginalist tradition originated by Sraffa's work reached important results, on a much wider front than is often recognised. Marginalist theoreticians were then pushed into concentrating their efforts into three fields. First we have intertemporal or temporary general equilibrium models, so general[10] as to be sterile as guidance for the interpretation of economic reality, in the sense that any event can be rationalised *ex post*, within these models, by assigning a particular set of values to the parameters, or by aptly changing these parameters. Second, we have disequilibrium models, requiring *ad hoc* assumptions on the adjustment mechanisms in order to obtain determinate results, and which often utilise an aggregate notion of capital. Finally, especially in the field of macroeconomics, both the theoretical debate[11] and the textbooks have fallen back on one-commodity models (with the misleading use of the label of general economic equilibrium models as soon as more than one single period is considered, as in overlapping generations models), surreptitiously forgetting the results of the capital theory debates recalled above, though never denying the validity of those critiques.[12]

The growing remoteness of such analyses from real world issues on the one side and from theoretical rigour on the other side opens the door to the revival of an approach alternative to the marginalist one: the classical approach strengthened by the assimilation of Keynes's ideas, as suggested at the end of the previous chapter. The development of such an alternative encounters different kinds of problems, concerning the clarification of the conceptual framework, the solution of specific analytical issues, the choice of an appropriate methodology. In the following sections we will consider these aspects, and the contributions already given in their respect within the alternative approach.

The rediscovery of the classical approach

Together with the critique of the marginalist theory, the second objective pursued by Sraffa – as already noted above – consists in reproposing the classical economists' approach, freed from the misunderstandings superimposed on it in decades of marginalist interpretations.

Sraffa's work for the critical edition of Ricardo's *Works and Correspondence* (Ricardo, 1951–55) begins in 1930, and goes on for more than a quarter of a century, interacting with the work on *Production of Commodities by Means of Commodities*. Sraffa's celebrated philological rigour is not pursued as an end in itself, but is the tool for bringing to the fore the very foundations of classical political economy. Because of this, the debate beginning in the 1970s on the Sraffian reconstruction of the history of economic thought is also part of the wider debate on the lines of development of economic science.

The attempt to deny that there is a specific classical approach to economics, distinct from the marginalist one, was already under way with Alfred Marshall (1961: Appendix i). As is well known, Marshall conceived the Ricardian analysis as one of the two pillars of the 'modern' theory of value and distribution: the pillar concerning the analysis of production costs, or supply curves, connected to the principle of the decreasing marginal productivity of land. The 'modern' theory, according to Marshall, completes the theoretical edifice with the second pillar, namely the analysis of demand curves based on the principle of decreasing marginal utility.

In a subtler way, Jacob Hollander (1904, 1910) tells the story of Ricardo's gradual retreat from a labour theory of value towards a theory of prices based on costs of production, which is considered open to the marginalist developments connected to the principle of decreasing marginal productivity, considered in turn a development of the 'Ricardian' theory of differential rent.

Marshall's and Jacob Hollander's views, here briefly recalled, were subjected to a devastating critique in Sraffa (1951). The interpretation of the classical approach as based on the notion of the surplus is in fact counterposed to their views. The reconstruction of the history of economic thought based on a clear-cut distinction between the classical and the marginalist approach, as proposed by Sraffa, is then developed in a long stream of writings – too numerous, especially in Italy, for it to be possible to recall all of them here.[13]

In opposition to this wide stream of literature (which embraces a variety of views, though on the common basis of the recognition of the central role of the surplus for the classical school, and of the distinction between the classical and marginalist approaches), some marginalist historians of economic thought re-proposed the thesis of a continuity of the two approaches. This thesis has twin implications: first, to deny the existence of a specific classical 'vision' of the economy; second, to depict once again the classicals as simple forerunners, rough and approximate in their analyses, of marginalist theories. Thus the debate in the history of economic thought appears as a central aspect of the more general debate opposing 'Sraffian' and 'marginalist' economists: an element at least as relevant as the strictly analytical one (namely, that concerning the theory of capital, recalled in the previous section). This explains the relevance of issues in the history of economic thought for the contemporary economics debate.

In this respect, let us recall Samuel Hollander's writings on classical economists, and the replies they received, both as far as a specific aspect is concerned (namely Ricardo's 'corn model'), and for a more general proposal of a 'marginalist' reading of Ricardo.[14] A subtler attempt at re-proposing as common to classical and marginalist economists 'at least' a view of value and distribution where the condition of the equality between demand and supply of capital and labour determines the equilibrium values for wage rate and rate of profits, is developed in different but substantially similar ways by various authors;[15] it can be maintained, however, that these interpretations too are based on a misreading of Ricardo, introducing elements that are extraneous to his thought.[16]

The debate, still under way, on the reconstruction of the history of economic thought thus plays a central role, and constitutes an integral part of the reconstruction of classical political economy started by Sraffa.

The analytical contributions stemming from Sraffa

Parallel to the utilisation of Sraffian results for the critique of authors and ideas central to the marginalist tradition, and to the reappraisal of classical political economy, the publication of Sraffa's book was followed by researches refining and developing his analysis of the relationships connecting relative prices to income distribution.

The first writings on Sraffa's book, leaving aside a long stream of reviews (some of which raise important issues), concern the translation of his analysis into mathematical terms.[17] The idea of substituting the assumption of a set of sectoral profit rates for Sraffa's assumption of a uniform rate of profits, suggested by Sylos Labini, was discussed and developed in a long stream of articles.[18] A problem raised by Newman (1962), concerning the possibility of non-positive prices for nonbasic commodities, is tackled and solved in an exchange of letters between Sraffa and Newman and in a few other writings.[19] The distinction between basic and nonbasic commodities is widely debated, up to the point of considering its applicability to problems of planning.[20] A number of writings focus on the standard commodity: the mathematical specification of its properties, some attempts at generalising it, and especially – as we will see in a later section – the possible use of that tool for solving the problem of the transformation of labour values into production prices, or in general for solving problems left unsolved within Marx's theory of value.

In the 1970s the work of analytical deepening shifts focus from the first to the second and third part of Sraffa's book. Two mathematical treatments of joint production are given by Lippi (1979) and Schefold (1989). The second of these authors then develops specific aspects, mainly concerning the choice of techniques and technical change, in a series of articles now collected in Schefold (1997). These writings are important not only for their analytical results, but also for the idea that Sraffa's analysis provides a better basis than traditional theory for the analysis of important practical issues, such as technological change, the energy issue and the ecological issue.

The treatment of both fixed capital and rent is developed and discussed in a long stream of articles.[21] The subsystem method, presented by Sraffa in a short appendix to his book, also received immediate attention.[22] As reconstructed by Pasinetti in terms of vertically integrated sectors, it came to be used recently as a tool for empirical analyses of productive inter-relations within the economy.[23] On the choice of techniques, apart from the debate raised by Levhari's 1965 article, and already recalled above, let us recall Bharadwaj (1989: Chapter 11), showing that the maximum number of points of 'switch of techniques' is equal to the number of basic commodities in the system.

A debate on the interpretation and the limits of Sraffa's analysis started in the late 1970s, revolving on the choice of techniques, especially with reference to the case of joint production. More specifically Steedman (1980a), followed – as indicated by Salvadori himself – by Salvadori (1979a), showed that the assumption of constant returns to scale is necessary for the treatment of the choice of techniques presented in Part Three of Sraffa, 1960; also, in the case of joint production difficulties appear for the identification of the cost minimising technology.[24] These results, especially the latter, lead Salvadori to suggest a blending of Sraffa's

(1960) and von Neumann's (1945–46) approaches, and a generalisation of the 'equations approach' into a 'weak inequalities approach'.[25] This debate is still open, and is crucial for the interpretation of Sraffa's analytical contribution. Here we will only recall that Sraffa himself stresses (Sraffa, 1960: v) that the statement concerning the absence of any assumption on returns to scale strictly speaking holds only for the First and Second Part of his book. There is thus a difference here with respect to Part Three that deals with the problem of the choice of techniques. Such a difference suggests that the analysis of the choice of techniques in Part Three of Sraffa's book, while essential for the critique of traditional marginalist theories of value and distribution, is not to be interpreted as providing the foundation for the analysis of how technical choice and technical change take place in the real world.[26]

The 'Ricardian' reconstruction: Pasinetti

When the attempts at reconstructing classical political economy go beyond the limits which Sraffa imposes on his book, and try to tackle the issues connected with the development of the economy over time, there is no unique path of research which can be logically deduced from Sraffa's analytical results; there is rather a multiplicity of lines of enquiry that are actively explored and confronted. In this and the following sections we will try to locate the distinguishing characteristics of three main lines of research along which different groups of economists try to proceed with the reconstruction of the Classical approach which Sraffa started.

A first wide-ranging development of Sraffa's analysis is that proposed in particular by Pasinetti in a number of writings, culminating in his 1981 volume on *Structural Change and Economic Growth*, subtitled *A Theoretical Essay on the Dynamics of the Wealth of Nations*.

Notwithstanding the reference to Adam Smith's *magnum opus* in the subtitle, Pasinetti's main reference is to Ricardian analysis. On methodological grounds, Pasinetti follows the principles of logical deduction, leaving to historical references a purely illustrative role: similarly to Ricardo and in direct opposition to Smith's predilection for historical generalisations as opposed to the analysis through models. Furthermore, Ricardo's 'model' is the subject of Pasinetti's 1965 growth model, which also incorporates Pasinetti's 1962 formulation of the post-Keynesian theory of distribution, connecting income distribution between wages and profits to the level of investments, once the saving propensities of workers and capitalists and the 'natural' growth rate are given. Subsequently, the development of the theory of vertically integrated sectors (Pasinetti, 1973) constitutes a decisive analytical step for moving on from the Sraffian analysis of the relationship between relative prices and income distribution to the analysis of economic growth. *Lectures on the Theories of Production* (Pasinetti, 1977a) can then also be considered as a reinterpretation of the history of economic thought, especially recent history (Sraffa, Leontief and von Neumann). This set of writings contributes to providing the basis for a specific view of the nature and role of economic science: a view which cannot be considered as opposed to that implicit in Sraffa's writings, but which can neither be identified with, nor logically deduced from, the latter.

A number of economists, especially Italians, side with Pasinetti in developing this line of enquiry. Let us recall at least the reappraisal of the history of economic thought proposed by Quadrio Curzio and Scazzieri (1984), based on the counter-position between the classical and the marginalist approaches as stemming from the distinction between the 'basic notion of reproducibility' and the 'basic notion of scarcity'. Let us also recall the studies of the Sraffian analysis of fixed capital considered as a premise for the analysis of growth (Baldone, 1974; Varri, 1974); and Marzi–Varri (1977) utilising (with recourse in their applied analysis to perhaps excessively simplified assumptions) the wage–profit frontier for the analysis of technical change.

As already noted, Pasinetti (1981) represents a synthesis of this line of research; hence we will refer to it in discussing the nature and limits of this line of enquiry.[27]

Pasinetti's purpose is 'to build a unifying theory behind all the new contributions to economics' (1981: 19): Kalecki and Keynes, the theory of the firm, Leontief and Sraffa, cycle theory, the Harrod–Domar model and the post-Keynesian distribution theories. Such a unifying theory has its main pillar 'not in the caprice and scarcity of Nature, but in the progress and ingenuity of Man', namely, not in the marginalist approach interpreted as the scarcity view, but in the classical approach interpreted as the reproducibility view (1981: 23).[28]

Proceeding from this basis Pasinetti aims to develop 'a theory which remains neutral with respect to the institutional organisation of society', concentrating attention on 'the "primary and natural" features' of the economic system, by which he means 'the conditions under which it may grow and take advantage of exploiting all its potential possibilities' (1981: 25). A model of non-proportional growth based on the full employment assumption is utilised for identifying such conditions, interpreted as 'necessary requirements for equilibrium growth' (1981: 25). Specifically, in any vertically integrated sector the 'natural' rate of profit – which differs from sector to sector – must be such as to ensure an amount of profits equal to the 'equilibrium' value of investments, that is, to the amount of investments required for expanding productive capacity at a rate equal to 'the rate of population growth' plus 'the rate of increase of per capita demand for each consumption good' (1981: 130). In order to explain the changes over time in the structure of demand, Pasinetti draws on 'Engel's law', thus avoiding any reference to subjective elements such as utility maps and consumers' preferences. The increase in per capita income and demand corresponds in equilibrium to the increase in per capita product due to technical progress (which can proceed at different speeds in different sectors).

In this context the notion of equilibrium assumes a *normative* meaning, linked as it is to the assumption of full utilisation of the available labour force and of productive capacity (see also 1981: 96–7, where the 'dynamic' equilibrium corresponds to the conditions allowing for continuous full employment over time). In other terms, Pasinetti's analysis focuses on what should happen to ensure full employment, not on the actual behaviour of an economic system necessarily tied to specific institutions.

From this viewpoint the issue of the relationship between the short and the long period is discussed: '*the very nature* of the process of long run growth requires a structural dynamics which leads to difficulties in the short run'. Hence the methodological suggestion 'of singling out first the fundamental structural dynamics which must take place and then of trying to facilitate them' (Pasinetti, 1981: 243–4): a suggestion which tends to affirm the priority of the normative analysis.

All this is not intended to deny the possibility and the usefulness of a direct analysis of short period issues, and more generally of the – certainly not optimal – way of functioning of concrete economies. In fact, various hints in Pasinetti's writings point in this direction.[29] But there is no doubt that, compared to the long-run 'normative' analysis discussed above, such hints are far less developed: they appear to constitute a second stage of analysis, subsequent to that decisive first stage which is the object of systematic formal analysis in Pasinetti's work.

Another aspect of Pasinetti's research concerns international economic relations. Among other things, the treatment of this theme allows us to see clearly a central element in which Pasinetti's views about the way of functioning of modern economies differ from those characterising classical political economy: the nature of the wealth of nations. Utilising his model, Pasinetti shows that 'trade' (i.e. the Ricardian principle of the exploitation of comparative advantages among the different countries involved in international trade) is 'a secondary source of international gain', while 'the primary source' is given by 'international learning' of technical knowledge (Pasinetti, 1981: 283 ff.). Hence the distinction hinted at above:

> In a pre-industrial society, wealth is mainly a stock of material goods – something that people have inherited from the past or have appropriated from 'nature' [...] But the wealth of an industrial nation is something quite different, or rather it is something deeper. It is not so much the material goods that people have; it is the technical knowledge on how to make them [...] If, in the pre-industrial world, the main way for a country to increase its wealth was to dominate and exploit its neighbours, today it has become to emulate them and do better.
>
> (Pasinetti, 1981: 275–6).

The 'Marxian' reconstruction: Garegnani

Some economists are convinced that the potentially most fruitful way to pursue the reconstruction of classical political economy along the line started by Sraffa consists in bringing to the fore, within the classical approach re-proposed by Sraffa, Marx's vision. As Garegnani (1981: 113) states, 'a revival of the Classical economists' theoretical approach cannot [...] take place but starting from the highest point of development which such an approach received in the past: the point which was reached with Marx'.

Naturally the Marx thus reproposed is a specific Marx: not necessarily a travesty, as many 'orthodox' Marxists maintained (see e.g. Medio, 1972); but certainly a Marx in which some elements are given emphasis, while others – though undoubtedly present in his writings, such as materialistic dialectic – are played down. Also, Sraffa's analytical contribution could not leave untouched Marx's 'vision' (in the wider sense of the term).

For example, the use of Sraffian analytical tools shows that the Marxian 'law of the falling rate of profit' is devoid of general validity.[30] Furthermore, contrary to what a number of authors have maintained, the standard commodity does not constitute an analytical tool capable of connecting the world of labour values to the world of production prices.[31] Finally, the widely debated problem of the 'transformation of labour values into production prices' is substantially solved, in the light of Sraffa's analytical results, by concluding that the results reached in terms of labour values are generally not confirmed by an analysis in terms of production prices.[32]

There were lengthy discussions on the precise measure in which this renewed Marx ('Marx after Sraffa', following the happy title of Steedman's 1977 iconoclastic book) corresponds to the original Marx.[33] At one extreme there are those, like Colletti (1968: 431), maintaining that 'Sraffa made a bonfire of Marx's analysis'. Among the various forms which this thesis took, a central element seems to be the idea that leaving aside dialectical materialism means leaving aside a central aspect of Marx's thought such as commodity fetishism.

To the contrary, some economists, and prominently Garegnani (1981, 1984), maintain that the differences between Sraffa's and Marx's analyses are not substantial. We are confronted rather with the development of one and the same paradigm, since Marx retains intact the analytical structure of classical economists centred on the notion of the surplus, which was then taken up by Sraffa with greater analytical rigour. In fact, the 'return to Marx' is considered to be precisely the road which Sraffa had in mind for the reconstruction of political economy. Marx's exploitation is considered as a fact of reality, as shown by the fact that the surplus generated in the productive process is at least partly appropriated, as profits and rents, by social classes different from the workers. Besides, the antagonistic relation between wages and profits – expressing on the plane of income distribution the class conflict opposing capitalists and workers – is said to be brought to the fore, with greatest clarity, by an analytical tool developed by Sraffa, the standard commodity. In fact, when the standard commodity is used as numeraire for measuring the wage rate, we get a negative linear relationship between wage rate and rate of profits. These foundations are considered sufficient for the central aspects of Marx's thought: 'the contingent nature of capitalism is demonstrated by Marx on the basis of an analytical nucleus consisting in what he often calls "the internal nexus of bourgeois economic relations", that is, basically, the antagonistic relation between wages and profits' (Garegnani, 1981: 112).

The analytical core common to classical economists, to Marx and Sraffa, is located by Garegnani[34] in the set of relations connecting production prices and distributive variables analysed in Sraffa (1960). More precisely:

> the surplus theories have [...] a *core* which is isolated from the rest of the analysis because the wage, the social product and the technical conditions of production appear there as already determined. It is in this 'core' that we find the determination of the shares other than wages as a residual: a determination which [...] will also entail the determination of the relative values of commodities. Further, as a natural extension of this, we shall find in the 'core' an analysis of the relations between, on the one hand, the real wage, the social product and the technical conditions of production (the independent variables) and, on the other hand, the shares other than wages constituting the surplus, and the relative prices (the dependent variables).
>
> (Garegnani, 1984: 296).

Two notes of caution are to be stressed. First, side by side with the relations considered *internal* to the core, the variables (both dependent and independent) can also be connected by other relations, which 'were left to be studied outside the "core"' (Garegnani, 1984: 297). Secondly, the notion of a core of the surplus theories remains substantially unchanged when the profit rate replaces the wage as the independent distributive variable determined exogenously, that is, outside the core (Garegnani, 1984: 321–2).

The dominant role attributed to the 'analytical core' which Marx shares with classical economists and Sraffa influences the line of enquiry followed in the reconstruction of political economy. The 'core' is taken as the foundation on which to rely in developing the analysis in different directions, corresponding to the elements considered as exogenous data in Sraffa's book (income distribution, production and employment levels, technology).

Furthermore, the analysis of the relations internal to the core and of those external to it are said to constitute 'distinct logical stages' (Garegnani, 1984: 297): the nature of the analysis is substantially different in the two cases. Garegnani (1990a: 124–5) characterises in a clear-cut way this difference. He points to a 'distinction between two fields of analysis: a field where general quantitative relations of sufficiently definite form can be postulated', i.e. the 'core'; 'and another field where relations in the economy are so complex and variable according to circumstances, as to allow not for general quantitative relations of sufficiently definite form', i.e. the rest of economic theory: 'The relations pertaining to this second field had accordingly to be studied in their multiplicity and diversity according to circumstances'.

At variance from what seems to be suggested by Pasinetti's contributions, Garegnani and his followers thus seem to interpret the analytical core common to Sraffa and classical economists not as a set of formal relations to be extended in 'more general' models, but rather as a set of relations of causes and effects that should constitute the foundations for the analyses of other aspects of economic life. More precisely, central relevance is attributed to the causal chain going from the wage rate, determined by socio-historical conditions (or alternatively by a profit rate determined by conventional and institutional factors explaining the interest rate), to relative prices and the second distributive variable, on the basis of a given technology. This core of causal relations constitutes the necessary reference point also when one proceeds to other parts of political economy, precisely because these relations are the only ones that can be considered as 'general quantitative relations'.

Another idea repeatedly defended by Garegnani (for instance, in Garegnani, 1990b) concerns the 'gravitation of market prices towards natural prices'. This idea raised a wide debate, which will be considered below. In fact the metaphor of gravitation, both imperfect and suggestive as are all metaphors, seems to be used by Garegnani mainly for stressing the relative 'stability' and 'persistence' of the elements (techniques in use, distribution) which are utilised to explain 'natural' prices, and along this road the point is reached of speaking of 'long period positions'. In this sense the idea of the gravitation of market prices towards natural prices helps to explain the central role attributed to the relations connecting economic variables within the 'core'. It is precisely this element – the central role of the 'core' – which characterises Garegnani's theoretical views, both in his interpretation of the connection between Sraffa and classical economists and Marx, and in his view of the line of research to be followed for the reconstruction of political economy initiated by Sraffa.

The 'Smithian' reconstruction: Sylos Labini

An interpretation of the central aspects of classical political economy different from those examined in the previous sections has been developed in a number of writings by Paolo Sylos Labini.[35] This line of research is characterised by the central role attributed to market forms, which are relatively overlooked by classical economists, in their interaction with the division of labour and the process of accumulation. This means bringing to the centre of the analysis a view of the process of capitalistic development which draws from Smith more than from Ricardo or Marx: a view based on the central role of the changes in the division of labour (or, more specifically, of technological change). From changes in the division of labour stem the changes over time in market forms and in the pace of accumulation. Developments in income distribution are then made to depend on these elements, together with aspects concerning public policy and the politico-institutional setting. In this way, while the notion of the surplus retains a central role in economic analysis, the functional relations connecting natural prices and income distribution lose their role as the central pillar of economic theorising.

More generally, Smith's vision of a development process characterised by both positive and negative elements, but fundamentally positive, is reproposed though in a somewhat different form by Sylos Labini (see for instance the proposal of a 'labour army' in Sylos Labini, 1974b). Sylos Labini's 'Smithian' vision is developed as an alternative, if not in opposition, to the traditional Marxian view of a progressive deterioration of capitalism (law of increasing misery, proletarisation, tendency to a falling rate of profits) up to the inevitable breakdown and the unavoidable revolutionary outcome.[36]

If confronted with the 'Smithian' vision of the reconstruction of political economy, Sraffa's contribution can be characterised exactly along the lines illustrated above, in Chapter 1: as a critique of the marginalist tradition; as a reconstruction of the classical conceptual apparatus; as a solution of the analytical problem constituting a crucial feeble point in the classical theoretical apparatus (the relationship connecting production prices and income distribution). This problem constituted then, and still constitutes, a crucial knot – in fact, *the* crucial one – for the construction of a theoretical system based on the notion of the surplus. However it did not constitute for classical economists, and should not constitute today, the main objective of economic enquiry. Such an objective should rather be located in the 'wealth of nations' and the factors determining its development over time and in different countries, especially the distribution of income and wealth (and – too often forgotten – the distribution of power, which has also to do with the role of market forms) among different groups of economic agents.

Sraffa's contribution is thus decisive for the vitality of the cultural project of reconstruction of classical political economy. However, it should also be recognised that in order to re-propose an interpretation of the development of the economic systems in which we live it is not sufficient to 'build on' the analysis developed by Sraffa in *Production of Commodities by Means of Commodities*: neither in the sense of gradually extending a basic formal model, nor in the sense of gradually extending a restricted analytical nucleus of causal relations. As a consequence, we should also recognise that the attempt to reconstruct classical political economy can – and should – be developed at least in certain aspects independently of Sraffa's contribution.

For instance, Sylos Labini (1962) revives the classical conception of market forms, based on the difficulty of entry of new firms into a sector rather than on the number of firms present in that sector, and analyses the factors determining the 'barriers to entry' facing new firms. Such factors are viewed as determining a deviation of the sectoral profit rate from the 'basic' profit rate that would prevail under free competition, i.e. in the case of unrestrained freedom of entry. Such an analysis of market forms is clearly compatible with the idea of a tendency to a uniform rate of profits in the case of free competition in all sectors of the economy, and is thus compatible with Sraffa's analysis: in comparison to the assumption of a uniform rate of profits, the introduction of non-competitive market forms can be considered as a 'second approximation'. But the objective of the analysis (namely, to locate the factors determining the size of the barriers to entry into the different sectors of the economy) can be pursued independently of an analysis of relative prices under competition such as the one conducted by Sraffa (1960). Among other things, it should be noted that a too direct link between the two lines of analysis, such as to attempt to enclose both of them simultaneously within the boundaries of a single mathematical model, would have the effect of limiting the horizon of the study of the barriers to entry uniquely to the determination of the sectoral profit rate differentials, since these represent the formal link connecting the analysis of market forms and the analysis of the relation between natural prices and income distribution. On the contrary, side by side with sectoral profit rate differentials and possibly more importantly, the analysis of market forms throws light on issues such as the influence of barriers to entry on the pace of technological change, on accumulation, on income distribution (especially when the nature of the barriers to entry and their level are different in the various sectors of the economy).[37]

The connection between the different lines of research contributing to the reconstruction of classical political economy (and in particular the connection between two lines of enquiry such as that on the relationship between relative prices and income distribution, and that on market forms) must be found in the reference to a common conceptual framework: the representation of the economy as a circular process, centred on the causes which allow the production of a surplus and determine its distribution among the different social classes and the different sectors of the economy and its utilisation. But we should also recognise that within this common conceptual framework it is possible to distinguish a whole series of analytical issues, obviously connected but best dealt with if subjected to separate analysis (though without losing sight – 'in the back of our minds', as Keynes said – of their interconnections).

The *analytical separability* of the different issues[38] opens the way to the use of *different analytical areas* for dealing with different analytical issues. The idea is rather widespread in modern science, with the noticeable exception of economics, where the dominant marginalist tradition favoured the idea that all problems should be dealt with through a unique method, namely constrained maximisation (or minimisation).[39] For instance, in the study of intelligence, the analysis of the interaction between symbols in the human mind is conducted in 'a different analytical area' from the analysis of the interaction of neurons in the human brain (Hofstaedter, 1979); but obviously the two analyses cannot belong to the same *corpus* if linked to two conflicting interpretations of human intelligence in general.

This short lapse into methodology is necessary for understanding how to solve, within the 'Smithian' approach, the problem of the relationship between what Garegnani calls 'the core' of classical political economy, and 'the rest of economic theory'. When the organisation of research in different analytical areas is recognised as possible and useful in dealing with different issues, the problem of *formal* consistency with the core cannot even be raised. Nor is it possible to state that the core constitutes a 'logically prior' stage in comparison to the 'logically subsequent' stages consisting in the treatment of other issues, contrary to what Garegnani implies. Moreover, as already said, there is no reason why the relations 'within the core' should constitute a privileged point of departure for the study of different economic issues (from technical change to accumulation). However, a *conceptual*, not a formal, consistency is required between the different theories developed for interpreting different aspects of economic reality, if such theories are to represent parts of a common *corpus* of doctrines. The relevance attributed to this kind of consistency (which at least partly explains the importance attributed to the debates concerning the history of economic thought: see Roncaglia, 1996) is connected to the fact that it constitutes the main defence against possible abuses of the idea of 'different analytical areas'.

It is only here that we find reasons for attributing a particularly important role to the set of analytical relations usually included in the field of the theory of value: it is within this field that the differences between different conceptions of the way of functioning of the economy most clearly appear, and can be expressed with the greatest precision. Clearly, from this point of view Sraffa's (1960) analytical contribution continues to play a central role also within what we have here called as the 'Smithian' reconstruction of classical political economy.

A preliminary evaluation of the three lines of enquiry

What has been said in the preceding pages does not imply basic contradictions between the three lines of enquiry – 'Ricardian', 'Marxian' and 'Smithian' – proposed for the reconstruction of classical political economy started by Sraffa. However, there are various differences. This section is concerned with some difficulties arising within the 'Ricardian' and 'Marxian' lines of enquiry, when interpreted as autonomous and counterposed to the 'Smithian' one.

Let us begin with the 'Ricardian' analysis developed in particular by Pasinetti. As we saw above, it is, at least in a first and fundamental stage, a *normative* analysis directed to determining the conditions of continuous full employment (or, in general, of a predetermined employment dynamics), in the presence of exogenous changes in labour forces, technology, consumers' tastes. The 'normative' character of Pasinetti's analysis stems from the fact that it has been developed in counter-position to the traditional marginalist view according to which market economies automatically tend to full employment. Within the marginalist tradition, full employment equilibrium is a position towards which the economy actually moves. Vice versa, the conditions of economic growth under continuous full employment analysed by Pasinetti are not automatically realised by market forces, but may constitute targets for policy interventions.

However, Pasinetti's model has also some limits from this point of view.[40] First, side by side with the assumption of full employment, decisive elements are determined from outside the model, such as, in particular, the parameters determining the pace of technical change. Second, even if we accept the point of view of the 'full employment planner', we still lack the second point of reference necessary to the planner's activity, namely an analysis of the tendencies of actual economic systems, when unhindered by intervention. It is precisely this latter kind of analysis which, in our opinion, constitutes the essence of political economy properly conceived. According to Pasinetti this kind of analysis represents a second stage, only hinted at in his work, logically subsequent to the analysis of what he calls the 'natural' properties of an economy, namely the conditions of growth under persistent full employment.

Concentrating the analysis on the *potentialities* of growth may tend by itself to obscure some aspects which are decisive for an understanding of the path actually followed by the economy. Let us briefly recall three such aspects: market forms, monetary and financial elements, the relationship between long and short run issues.

First aspect: market forms can differ from sector to sector and can be modified, within each sector, by the very process of development. As we saw above (pp. 94–5), some economists attribute to market forms a decisive influence on the actual tendencies of development of different economic systems. However, the analysis of vertically integrated sectors leaves on a secondary plane the possible differences in market forms in the various industries which are then recombined in varying proportions between hypothetical vertically integrated sectors. In consequence each vertically integrated sector has different market forms inside it; so that strategic behavioural differences between different sectors, which may influence the shape of economic development, are obscured.

The second aspect consists in the limited and largely passive role played by monetary and financial factors in Pasinetti's (1981: Chapter 8) analysis. These factors are, in fact, relegated to that second stage of research which should follow the analysis of the 'natural' properties of an economic system. This is a logical corollary of the line of enquiry privileged by Pasinetti: in his analysis the potentialities of development are defined by 'real' factors such as the growth of population, the pace of productivity and the choices of final consumers; while monetary factors do not play any role on this account. Vice versa, economists within the Keynesian tradition usually, and rightly, stress the relevance of these latter factors in determining the actual path of economic development.

The third aspect consists in the link between short and long-run problems. In Pasinetti's analysis the former stem from the latter. However, the opposite procedure – namely considering long-run problems as stemming from short run ones – appears, at least in some cases, as more appropriate to the analysis of the evolution of actual economic systems. This holds especially for the employment issue, which is the central objective of Pasinetti's analysis: 'Keynesian' short run unemployment, due to short run insufficiency of effectual demand, implies under-utilisation of available productive capacity, and thus negatively influences investments intended to enlarge productive capacity; as a consequence, the latter may maintain an insufficient pace to balance the growth of population and technical progress (see Roncaglia, 1988: Section 6). Technical change itself, which in Pasinetti's analysis is considered as an exogenous factor, is in fact influenced by the actual path of investments and production.

The assumption of continuous full employment, which is the central pillar of Pasinetti's analysis, also constitutes the premise for the idea recalled above (pp. 87–8) according to which the international learning of technical knowledge constitutes the primary source of advantages stemming from international economic relations. These latter, in fact, also influence the degree of utilisation of available productive capacity and the pace of accumulation in the different countries: it is only the assumption of continuous full employment which allows us to neglect these aspects, and to concentrate attention uniquely on the evolution of technical knowledge. Once this is recognised, the contrast perceived by Pasinetti between his own notion of wealth of nations and the traditional one falls. Undeniably, the classical notion attributes a central role to technical knowledge in explaining the wealth of nations (think, for example, of the Smithian analysis of the division of labour). At the same time, side by side with the stage reached by technical knowledge one has to keep in view, precisely as classical economists used to do, the 'material' aspect of the wealth of nations as well, namely the actual path of production, once the possibility of a difference between such a path and the potential full employment one is recognised. In other terms, the notion of the wealth of nations proposed by Pasinetti, in so far as it concentrates attention *exclusively* on technical knowledge, is connected to the normative orientation of his analysis, focused on the identification of the conditions of persistent full employment. Instead, the classical (Smithian) notion of wealth of nations recognises the relevance of technical knowledge side by side with other elements in determining the actual path of development of economic systems.

Of course, these remarks do not deny the usefulness of a 'normative' analysis, such as that developed by Pasinetti. Rather, they point to the desirability that, side by side with such analysis, and not as a second and logically subsequent stage, a central role be given also, and perhaps mainly, to analyses of actual economic events.

Let us now proceed to examine the second line of enquiry illustrated above, namely the 'Marxian' one developed in particular by Garegnani. Here we will leave aside, as not relevant to our purposes, the philological issue concerning the correctness of Garegnani's interpretation of Marx's thought. We will rather concentrate attention on two related aspects, decisive for this line of enquiry: the notion of 'the core of the surplus theories', and the notion of the 'gravitation of market prices towards natural prices'.

This latter thesis in particular has been the object of a long debate. Various economists stressed that, as a matter of fact, natural prices do not remain unchanged over the time span necessary to the completion of the gravitation process of market prices towards natural prices; the 'natural position' may or may not be reached depending on the assumptions adopted concerning the pace of change of the elements determining the natural prices, on the one side, and the speed of the adjustment of market to natural prices, on the other side.[41] Additional difficulties arise when it is admitted that the path followed by market prices may influence the elements (technique in use, income distribution) determining natural prices. Other economists stressed that gravitation requires strict formal conditions, through analyses where market prices are treated as theoretical variables determined by supply and demand conditions, and where supply and/or demand respond to divergences between market and natural prices.[42] Such a notion of market prices is necessary when one attributes to gravitation the meaning of a theory concerning the level of market prices and their path over time. But such a notion cannot be attributed either to classical economists or to Sraffa: for them, market prices represent the exchange ratios actually observable in reality, influenced by a multiplicity of factors, both systematic and unsystematic, while natural prices indicate the theoretical variable expressing the action of those factors alone on which the economist chooses to focus attention.[43]

However, as we have already hinted, the thesis concerning gravitation of market towards natural prices is not necessarily to be interpreted as a precise *theory* of market prices. The analysis of the relationship between market and natural prices may be pursued not by trying to theorise the path actually followed by market prices, but rather by pointing to the direction of their movement, towards – or away from – natural prices; precisely in this way we should interpret the classical (Smithian) theory of competition, according to which any deviation of market from natural prices provokes reactions on the side of economic agents leading market towards natural prices. When interpreted in this way, the thesis of gravitation comes out as nothing but a different name for the classical theory of competition.

Garegnani, however, seems to add two other elements: first, the idea, already hinted at, that the elements determining natural prices are 'persistent', that is, relatively stable, so that the speed of movement of natural prices, due to exogenous changes in the factors determining them, would turn out to be significantly lower than the speed of movement of market prices in their process of competitive adjustment towards natural prices; second, the idea, which is a corollary of the first, that natural prices, and hence their determinants, are (or can be considered) independent of short period movements in market prices. Both these ideas, as noted above, have been disputed in the course of the debate concerning gravitation. (In that debate – as in so many other occasions – two aspects were sometimes confused: first, whether these ideas represent more or less faithfully the classical economists' views; second – what is relevant here – whether they are useful in representing the way of working of contemporary economic systems.)

These critiques hit the central aspect of the thesis of gravitation, namely the 'strong' characterisation of the idea of 'persistence'. In fact, according to the thesis of gravitation, the forces regulating the process of economic reproduction would be persistent, not only in the commonly accepted sense that their mode of action is persistent and systematic, but in the stricter sense of attributing persistence (stability) to the quantitative expression (the 'levels') of the factors determining the system of relative prices. Specifically, persistence (stability) is thus attributed to technology and the corresponding levels of production, which – together with the system of natural prices they imply – constitute the 'long period positions' towards which actual economic systems are said to gravitate).

Together with this 'strong' notion of gravitation, Garegnani's line of enquiry is characterised by the central role attributed to the 'analytical core of the surplus theories'. As we saw above (pp. 90–1), Garegnani attributes logical priority to the 'analytical core', in the sense that only within it is it possible to identify 'general quantitative relations' connecting economic variables. In some respects, this idea resembles – even if the boundaries of the analytical core are different – Pasinetti's idea discussed above concerning the two stages of analysis among which priority is attributed to the one analysing the 'natural' properties of the economy. When pushed to its extreme limits, this distinction between the 'analytical core' and the rest of economic analysis tends to coincide with the distinction between *economic theory* and *political economy* as proposed by Lunghini (1975) in his interpretation of Sraffa: a distinction by which Lunghini wants to show how limited the scope of constructive theoretical reasoning is in the economic field.

We can thus understand how the idea of gravitation, together with that of the central, logically prior and theoretically dominating role attributed to the 'analytical core', may constitute an obstacle to the analysis of issues such as technical change, or the link connecting division of labour, market forms and income distribution.

What has been said in the preceding section suggests that another interpretation of Sraffa's analysis (developed in Roncaglia, 1978, and re-proposed in synthesis in Chapter 2 above) may be preferable, being based on a 'weaker' notion of natural prices, considered as the theoretical outcome of the action of certain forces 'isolated *in vacuo*', since they are considered as those influencing exchange ratios in a systematic way (while giving up any attempt at *proving* that the selection of such forces is the correct one, since such an attempt is considered as methodologically unwarranted). Such an interpretation of Sraffa's analytical contribution may seem more restricted than the one based on the 'strong' notion of gravitation and on the attribution to the 'analytical core' of a central and logically prior role; but in fact it turns out to be more fruitful in overcoming the barrier built by Garegnani between the 'general quantitative relations' and 'the rest of economic theory'. As suggested (pp. 95–6), different 'analytical pieces' may coexist within a common process of theoretical reconstruction, once the possibility of 'different analytical areas' is recognised for the analysis of different aspects of the functioning of economic systems, and if we avoid attributing too rigid a meaning to the central role inevitably assigned within the theoretical debate to the classical problem of value, as a decisive aspect for distinguishing between different economic 'visions'.

Once again it may be useful to stress that these remarks refer to specific aspects of Garegnani's contribution, and not to the central idea of a very strict link between Sraffa's analysis and classical political economy, nor to the objective of a reconstruction of classical political economy as an alternative to the marginalist approach. In the case of the 'Marxian' approach as in the case of the 'Ricardian' one, the critical remarks illustrated in the present section concern some aspects of the lines of research proposed for the reconstruction of economic theory, and not the general vision underlying such a reconstruction.

Let us summarise the results of our reasoning. We saw, in the preceding sections, that there are different lines of enquiry which, stemming more or less directly from Sraffa's contributions, tend to a reconstruction of classical political economy. However, this does not imply that such lines of enquiry are mutually exclusive: that is, that only one among them may offer a positive ground for the work of reconstruction, while all the others would lead to closed alleys. Following the 'Smithian' line of enquiry proposed in particular by Sylos Labini, and accepting the possible coexistence of different analytical areas, we may find useful elements for the reconstruction of classical political economy in each of the different lines of enquiry discussed above, provided of course that we recognise the limits of each. Thus, for instance, Pasinetti's analysis can be recognised as the analysis of a specific issue (the conditions for growth under continuous full employment, and their implications), rather than as a 'general model' of the functioning of an economy; specifically, we have to recognise the difference between the meaning that the notion of 'natural values' has in the context of Pasinetti's analysis and in the classical tradition. Analogously, various aspects of Garegnani's contributions are useful for the reconstruction of political economy, provided that his thesis of a supremacy of the relations analysed within the 'core' in comparison to those external to it (implying that the analysis of relations of the second group should stem from the first group of relations) is abandoned. At the same time, the 'Smithian' line of enquiry itself cannot but gain in clarity and analytical robustness by giving stronger attention to its links with the classical surplus approach and with Sraffa's analytical contributions.

Conclusions

Let us briefly summarise the path followed in this chapter. The first step consisted in providing a synthetic survey of the debates stemming from Sraffa's writings. Such debates followed three main lines, which have been discussed separately: the critique of traditional marginalist theory, the reconstruction of the history of economic thought and in particular of the conceptual and analytical framework of classical political economy, the mathematical treatment and extension of the analytical propositions developed by Sraffa in *Production of Commodities by Means of Commodities*.

The second step consisted in a summary illustration of what we may consider to be the main attempts at reconstructing classical political economy. Thus, we discussed the 'Ricardian' line of enquiry developed by Pasinetti and others; the 'Marxian' line of enquiry attributable primarily to Garegnani; the 'Smithian' line of enquiry mainly originating from Sylos Labini's writings.

Finally, the third step consisted in offering some critical remarks on the difficulty that the project of reconstructing classical political economy would meet, if either of the first two lines of enquiry were considered as autonomous and self-contained. Clearly, this part of our work more than others reflects the direct participation of the present writer in the debate. The conclusion suggested to the reader is that the most fruitful line of enquiry for the reconstruction of classical political economy would imply integrating within the 'Smithian' approach some important original contributions developed within the 'Ricardian' and 'Marxian' approaches, while rejecting the idea that they should be developed in a self-contained way, or the idea that they should be considered as superior to the other lines of enquiry.

Here we cannot try to sketch the setting which could emerge from a critical synthesis of the different lines of enquiry stemming from Sraffa's contribution. It is clear, in any case, that while the reconstruction of classical political economy can be said to be well under way, much difficult work still remains to be done (also because economists analyse a continuous changing reality, requiring a continuous adaptation of the theoretical apparatus itself). It is precisely for this reason that economic research today, in particular within the revival of the classical approach, far from going through a crisis, is a lively and fascinating enterprise.

Notes

1 Samuelson's theses were refuted by Garegnani, 1970a, and by Spaventa, 1968; Levhari's by Pasinetti, 1966, followed by various other authors, among which let us recall Garegnani, 1966; Samuelson, 1966, and Levhari (with Samuelson, 1966) themselves recognise the erroneous nature of their thesis. This notwithstanding, in the following years some skirmish still takes place, without however adding anything to the results of the previous debate: see for instance Gallaway and Shukla, 1974 and Garegnani, 1976; Burmeister, 1977, 1979 and Pasinetti 1979a, 1979b.
2 See Bliss, 1970; Hahn, 1982.
3 See Garegnani, 1970b, 1979, 1985; Roncaglia, 1978: Chapter 6; and more recently Kurz and Salvadori, 1995: Chapter 14; Schefold, 1997: Chapter 18.
4 See Steedman, 1989: Chapter 8 on Jevons; Steedman, 1992 on Wicksteed.
5 See Solow, 1963, 1969 and Pasinetti, 1969; for the discussion which followed Pasinetti's critiques, see then Solow, 1970 and Pasinetti, 1970; Dougherty, 1972 and Pasinetti, 1972.
6 See for example the readings edited by Steedman, 1977b, 1979a; and Steedman, 1979b.
7 See respectively Steedman, 1989: Chapter 11; 1985a, 1985b. Deep-reaching critiques of the theory of consumer's choice have been developed also by Parrinello, 1982a.
8 These critiques, hinted at in Garegnani, 1964–65, have been developed in Roncaglia and Tonveronachi, 1978, 1985, and in Roncaglia, 1988.

9   See most recently Forni and Lippi, 1997.

10 Notwithstanding the adoption of highly restrictive assumptions, such as that of convexity (namely, decreasing returns) both in production and in consumption.

11 To give just two examples, think of the theory of real cycles, or the so-called 'new growth theory'.

12 Occasionally the recourse to analytical tools such as the aggregate production function is justified with the distinction between 'highbrow theories', internally consistent but wholly irrelevant on the practical level, and 'low-brow theories', relevant for practical matters but based on foundations already recognised as mistaken. In this latter case, the use of more or less advanced mathematical tools should not lead us to forget, as unfortunately too often it happens, that these contributions are precisely 'low-level' contributions, which as such should be excluded from the field of economic science.

13 Let us recall at least Maurice Dobb's (1973) synthesis, and Krishna Bharadwaj's researches focused on the transition stage from the classical to the marginalist approach (Bharadwaj, 1978, and 1989: Chapter 6). For some further references, see Roncaglia, 1990a.

14 See Hollander, 1973a, 1973b, 1975, 1979, 1987, 1997; for the critique to his thesis on the non-existence of the corn model attributed to Ricardo, see Eatwell 1975a and Garegnani 1982; for the critique to his thesis of a 'marginalist' Ricardo, see Roncaglia, 1982. Peach (1984, 1993) criticises both the defence of the corn-model on the side of Eatwell and Garegnani, and the thesis of a 'marginalist' Ricardo proposed by Hollander.

15 See Casarosa, 1974, 1978, 1982; Hicks and Hollander, 1977; Caravale and Tosato, 1980.

16 See Roncaglia 1982: 347–50, 373; Rosselli 1985; and, along partly different lines, Pasinetti 1982.

17 See Newman, 1962, for the case of simple production; Manara, 1968, for the case of joint production; see then the wide treatments of Pasinetti, 1975; Abraham-Frois and Berrebi, 1976, and, more recently, the careful analysis by Kurz and Salvadori, 1995.

18 Let us recall here Parrinello, 1982b, and Steedman, 1989: Chapter 6. On this as on other issues touched on in this section, see the bibliography in Roncaglia, 1978, which lists the works connected to the different aspects of the Sraffian analysis published up to 1977. See also the readings edited by Pasinetti, 1977b, Steedman, 1988, Salvadori and Steedman, 1990.

19 Recalled in Roncaglia, 1978: 62–4, to which we refer for an interpretation of the economic meaning of the mathematical debate. The exchange of letters between Sraffa and Newman is published in Bharadwaj, 1989: Chapter 11.

20 For a synthetic survey and evaluation of this debate, see Roncaglia, 1990c, which also provides an assessment of the relevance of Sraffa's analysis for applied economics.

21 A number of papers on fixed capital are collected in Salvadori, 1981. On the theory of rent let us recall at least Quadrio Curzio, 1967; Montani, 1972; Kurz, 1990: Chapter 6.

22 See Harcourt and Massaro, 1964, Zaghini, 1967, and especially Pasinetti, 1973.

23 See Momigliano and Siniscalco, 1982, 1984.

24 See Salvadori, 1979b, 1982, and, independently, Bidard, 1984.

25 See Salvadori, 1979b, introduction to 1981, 1982: 295, and in particular 1985; among the most recent contributions, see Kurz and Salvadori 1995: Chapter 13.

26 See pp. 48–51 above.

27 For further developments, see then Pasinetti, 1988, 1990, 1993. In an at least partly analogous direction, but focusing attention on the role of scarce resources and hence of rent in the analysis of economic dynamics in the presence of technological change, see Quadrio Curzio (1967, 1975, and with Pellizzari, 1996).

28 On the limits of this interpretation of the marginalist and classical approaches, see Roncaglia, 1978: 5–6, 124–6.

29 See Pasinetti, 1981, and particularly the final four chapters; 1993.

30 See Steedman, 1977a: Chapter 9; the problem is discussed in various papers collected in Screpanti and Zenezini, 1978.

31 See Meek, 1961; Medio, 1972; Eatwell, 1975b and, for a critique, Roncaglia, 1978: 76–9.

32 See in particular Steedman, 1977a; for a history of the transformation problem, see for instance Vicarelli, 1975.

33 For a bibliography of this debate, see Roncaglia, 1978: 161–6. Let us recall in particular Lippi's book, 1978, and more recently the wide collection of essays edited by Caravale, 1991.

34 See the essays collected in Garegnani, 1981, 1984, 1990.

35 See Sylos Labini, 1954, 1962, 1974a, 1974b, 1977, 1983, 1984.

36 This counter-position is particularly clear in Sylos Labini's writings on social classes (1974b) and on underdevelopment (1983); for a direct critique of the Marxian 'vision', see Sylos Labini, 1994: 3–24.

37 See Sylos Labini, 1962, 1974a, 1984.

38 Let us recall that this 'separability' is suggested in Roncaglia, 1978: Chapter 7, as a possible interpretation of the method implicit in Sraffa, 1960; see above, Chapter 2: 55–60.

39 This is for instance the main thesis of Samuelson's *Foundations*: see Samuelson, 1947: 3.

40 See Shapiro, 1984, and Pasinetti's reply, Pasinetti, 1984.

41 See in particular Parrinello, 1977. We may think, for instance, to the extremely speedy technological change in sectors such as that of personal computers, in counter-position to the near-staticity of other sectors; let us recall, in this context, that natural (or production) prices are relative prices, as such dependent on the relative difficulty of production of the different commodities (and on income distribution).

42 See for instance Arena, 1981; Steedman, 1989: Chapter 6; Boggio, 1985.

43 See Roncaglia, 1990.

References

Abraham-Frois, G. and Berrebi, E. (1976) *Théorie de la valeur, des prix et de l'accumulation,* Paris: Economica.

Arena, R. (1981) 'A propos de la convergence des prix courants vers les prix naturels', *Cahiers d'économie politique,* 6: 53–75.

Babbage, C. (1832) *On the Economy of Machinery and Manufactures,* London.

Baldone, S. (1974) 'Il capitale fisso nello schema teorico di Piero Sraffa', *Studi economici,* 29: 45–106.

Baranzini, M. (ed.) (1982) *Advances in Economic Theory,* Oxford: Blackwell.

Becattini, G. (1989) 'Riflessioni sul distretto industriale marshalliano come concetto socio-economico', *Stato e mercato,* 25: 111–28.

Bellofiore, R. (ed.) (1986) *Tra teoria economica e grande cultura europea: Piero Sraffa,* Milan: Franco Angeli.

Bharadwaj, K. (1978) *Classical Political Economy and Rise to Dominance of Supply and Demand Theories,* Calcutta: Orient Longman.

—— (1989) *Themes in Value and Distribution,* London: Unwin Hyman.

Bharadwaj, K. and Schefold, B. (eds) (1990) *Essays on Piero Sraffa,* London: Unwin Hyman.

Bidard, C. (1984) 'Choix techniques en production jointe', in C. Bidard (ed.), *La production jointe,* Paris: Economica.

Bliss, C.J. (1970) 'Comment on Garegnani', *Review of Economic Studies,* 37: 437–8.

Böhm-Bawerk, E. von (1889) *Kapital und Kapitalzins. Zweite Abteilung: Positive Theorie des Kapitales,* Innsbruck.

Boffito, C. (1973) *Teoria della moneta,* Turin: Einaudi.

Boffito, C. (1973) *Teoria della moneta*, Turin: Einaudi.

Boggio, L. (1985) 'On the stability of production prices', *Metroeconomica*, 37: 241–67.

Burmeister, E. (1977) 'On the social significance of the reswitching controversy', *Revue d'économie politique*, 87: 330–50.

—— (1979) 'Professor Pasinetti's "unobtrusive postulate", regular economies, and the existence of a well-behaved aggregate production function', *Revue d'économie politique*, 89: 644–52.

Caravale, G. (ed.) (1991) *Marx and Modern Economic Analysis*, 2 vols, Aldershot: Edward Elgar.

Caravale, G. and Tosato, D. (1980) *Ricardo and the Theory of Value, Distribution and Growth,* London: Routledge.

Casarosa, C. (1974) 'La teoria ricardiana della distribuzione e dello sviluppo economico', *Rivista di politica economica*, 44: 959–1015.

—— (1978) 'A new formulation of the Ricardian system', *Oxford Economic Papers*, 30: 38–63.

—— (1982) 'The new view of the Ricardian theory of distribution and economic growth', in M. Baranzini (ed.), *Advances in Economic Theory*, Oxford: Blackwell.

Chamberlin, E. (1933) *The Theory of Monopolistic Competition*, Cambridge, MA: Harvard University Press.

Ciocca, P. and Rinaldi, R. (1997) 'L'inflazione in Italia, 1914–20. Considerazioni a margine della tesi di laurea di Piero Sraffa', *Rivista di storia economica*, 13: 3–40.

Clapham, J.A. (1922) 'Of empty economic boxes', *Economic Journal*, 32: 305–14.

Colletti, L. (1968) *Il marxismo ed Hegel*, Bari: Laterza.

Corsi, M. (1991) *Division of Labour, Technical Change and Economic Growth*, Aldershot: Avebury.

De Cecco, M. (1993) 'Piero Sraffa's "Monetary inflation in Italy during and after the war": an introduction', *Cambridge Journal of Economics*, 17: 1–5.

Dobb, M. (1973) *Theories of Value and Distribution since Adam Smith*, Cambridge: Cambridge University Press.

Dougherty, C.R.S. (1972) 'On the rate of return and the rate of profit', *Economic Journal*, 82: 1324–50.

Eatwell, J. (1975a) 'The interpretation of Ricardo's Essay on Profits', *Economica*, 42: 182–7.

—— (1975b) 'Mr. Sraffa's standard commodity and the rate of exploitation', *Quarterly Journal of Economics*, 89: 543–55.

Einaudi, L. (1931) 'Per una nuova collana di economisti', *La riforma sociale*, 7–8: 394–9.

Faucci, R. (1986) 'Fra Einaudi e Gramsci: Sraffa e la cultura economica italiana degli anni venti', in R. Bellofiore (ed.), *Tra teoria economica e grande cultura europea: Piero Sraffa*, Milan: Franco Angeli.

Fausti, L. (1998) *Intelletti in dialogo. Antonio Gramsci e Piero Sraffa*, Celleno (VT): Fondazione Guido Piccinni e La Piccola Editrice.

Fiori, G. (1997) *Una storia italiana. Vita di Ernesto Rossi*, Turin: Einaudi.

Forni, M. and Lippi, M. (1997) *Aggregation and the Microfoundations of Dynamic Macroeconomics*, Oxford: Clarendon Press.

Gallaway, L. and Shukla, V. (1974) 'The neoclassical production function', *American Economic Review*, 64: 348–58.

Garegnani, P. (1960) *Il capitale nelle teorie della distribuzione*, Milan: Giuffrè.

—— (1964–65) 'Note su consumi, investimenti e domanda effettiva', *Economia internazionale*, reprinted in Garegnani (1979).

—— (1966) 'Switching of techniques', *Quarterly Journal of Economics*, 80: 554–67.

—— (1970a) 'Heterogeneous capital, the production function and the theory of distribution', *Review of Economic Studies*, 37: 407–36.

—— (1970b) 'A reply', *Review of Economic Studies*, 37: 439.

—— (1976) 'The neoclassical production function: comment', *American Economic Review*, 66: 424–7.

—— (1979) *Valore e domanda effettiva*, Turin: Einaudi.

—— (1981) *Marx e gli economisti classici*, Turin: Einaudi.

—— (1982) 'On Hollander's interpretation of Ricardo's early theory of profits', *Cambridge Journal of Economics*, 6: 65–77.

—— (1984) 'Value and distribution in the classical economists and Marx', *Oxford Economic Papers*, 36: 291–325.

—— (1988) 'Actual and normal magnitudes: a comment on Asimakopulos', *Political Economy*, 4: 251–8.

—— (1990a) 'Sraffa: Classical versus Marginalist analysis', in K. Bharadwaj and B. Schefold (eds).

—— (1990b) 'On some supposed obstacles to the tendency of market prices towards natural prices', *Political Economy*, 6: 329–59.

Gerratana, V. (1991) 'Gramsci e Sraffa', in V. Gerratana (ed.), *P. Sraffa, Lettere a Tania per Gramsci*, Rome: Editori Riuniti.

Ginzburg, A. (1986) 'Sraffa e Keynes su inflazione e deflazione', in R. Bellofiore (ed.), *Tra teoria economica e grande cultura europea: Piero Sraffa*, Milan: Franco Angeli.

Gramsci, A. (1975) *Quaderni del carcere*, edited by V. Gerratana, 4 vols, Turin: Einaudi.

Gramsci, A. and Sraffa, P. (1924) 'Problemi di oggi e di domani', *Ordine nuovo*, 1–15 apr., 1: 4.

Hahn, F. (1982) 'The Neo-Ricardians', *Cambridge Journal of Economics*, 6: 353–74.

Harcourt, G.C. (1972) *Some Cambridge Controversies in the Theory of Capital*, Cambridge: Cambridge University Press.

Harcourt, G.C. and Massaro, V.C. (1964) 'A note on Mr. Sraffa's subsystems', *Economic Journal*, 74: 715–22.

Harrod, R. (1951) *The Life of John Maynard Keynes*, London: Macmillan.

—— (1961) 'Review of P. Sraffa, Production of Commodities by Means of Commodities', *Economic Journal*, 71: 783–7.

Hayek, F. von (1931a) *Prices and Production*, London: Routledge.

—— (1931b) 'Reflections on the pure theory of money of Mr. J.M. Keynes', *Economica*, 11: 270–95 (reprinted in Hayek 1995, vol. IX).

—— (1932) 'Money and capital: a reply', *Economic Journal*, 42: 237–49.

—— (1995) *Contra Keynes and Cambridge*, edited by B. Caldwell, *Collected Works*, vol. IX, Chicago: University of Chicago Press.

Hicks, J. and Hollander, S. (1977) 'Mr. Ricardo and the moderns', *Quarterly Journal of Economics*, 91: 351–69.

Hofstaedter, D.R. (1979) *Gödel, Escher, Bach*, New York: Basic Books.

Hollander, J. (1904) 'The development of Ricardo's theory of value', *Quarterly Journal of Economics*, 18: 455–91.

—— (1910) *David Ricardo – A Centenary Estimate*, Baltimore (reprinted by New York: McKelley, 1968).

—— (1973a) *The Economics of Adam Smith*, Toronto: University of Toronto Press.

—— (1973b) 'Ricardo's analysis of the profit rate, 1813–15', *Economica*, 40: 260–82.

—— (1975) 'Ricardo and the corn profit model: reply to Eatwell', *Economica*, 42: 188–202.

—— (1979) *The Economics of David Ricardo*, Toronto: University of Toronto Press.

—— (1987) *Classical Economics*, Toronto: University of Toronto Press.

—— (1997) *The Economics of Thomas Robert Malthus*, Toronto: University of Toronto Press.

Jevons, W.S. (1879) *The Theory of Political Economy*, 2nd edition, London.

Johnson, H.G. (1962) 'Review of "Production of Commodities by Means of Commodities"', *Canadian Journal of Economics and Political Science*, 28: 464–5.

Kaldor, N. (1934) 'The equilibrium of the firm', *Economic Journal*, 44: 60–76.

—— (1972) 'The irrelevance of equilibrium economics', *Economic Journal*, 82: 1237–55.

Keynes, J.M. (1913) *Indian Currency and Finance*, London: Macmillan.

—— (1923) *Tract on Monetary Reform*, London: Macmillan.

—— (1930) *A Treatise on Money*, 2 vols, London: Macmillan.

—— (1931) 'The pure theory of money. A reply to Dr. Hayek', *Economica*: 9, 387–97 (reprinted in Hayek 1995, vol. IX).

—— (1933) *Thomas Robert Malthus*, in *Essays in Biography*, London: Macmillan.

—— (1936) *General Theory of Employment, Interest and Money*, London: Macmillan.

—— (1973) *The General Theory and After*, vol. XIII (*Part I: Preparation*) and vol. XIV (*Part II: Defence and Development*), *The Collected Writings of John Maynard Keynes*, London: Macmillan.

—— (1979) *The General Theory and After. A Supplement*, *The Collected Writings of John Maynard Keynes*, vol. XXIX, London: Macmillan.

Keynes, J.M. and Sraffa, P. (eds) (1938) *An Abstract of "A Treatise of Human Nature"*, 1740, by David Hume, Cambridge: Cambridge University Press.

Kregel, J.A. (1976) 'Economic methodology in the face of uncertainty: the modelling methods of Keynes and the Post-Keynesians', *Economic Journal*, 86: 209–25.

—— (1983) 'Effective demand: origins and development of the notion', in J.A. Kregel (ed.), *Distribution, Effective Demand and International Economic Relations*, London: Macmillan.

Kuhn, T. (1962) *The Structure of Scientific Revolutions*, Chicago: Chicago University Press.

Kurz, H. (1990) *Capital, Distribution and Effective Demand*, Cambridge: Polity Press.

Kurz, H. and Salvadori, N. (1995) *Theory of Production. A Long Period Analysis*, Cambridge: Cambridge University Press.

Levhari, D. (1965) 'A nonsubstitution theorem and switching of techniques', *Quarterly Journal of Economics*, 79: 98–105.

Levhari, D. and Samuelson, P. (1966) 'The nonswitching theorem is false', *Quarterly Journal of Economics*, 80: 518–19.

Lippi, M. (1978) *Value and Naturalism in Marx*, London: New Left Books.

—— (1979) *I prezzi di produzione*, Bologna: il Mulino.

Lunghini, G. (1975) 'Teoria economica ed economia politica: note su Sraffa', in G. Lunghini (ed.), *Produzione, capitale e distribuzione*, Milan: Isedi.

Malcolm, N. (1958) *Ludwig Wittgenstein: a Memoir*, Oxford: Oxford University Press.

Manara, C. (1968) 'Il modello di Piero Sraffa per la produzione congiunta di merci a mezzo di merci', *L'industria*, 1: 3–18.

Marshall, A. (1961) *Principles of Economics*, variorum ed., London: Macmillan.

Marzi, G. and Varri, P. (1977) *Variazioni di produttività nell' economia italiana: 1959–1967*, Bologna: il Mulino.

Medio, A. (1972) 'Profits and surplus value: appearance and reality in capitalist production', in E.K. Hunt and J.G. Schwartz (eds), *A Critique of Economic Theory*, Harmondsworth: Penguin.

Meek, R. (1961) 'Mr. Sraffa's rehabilitation of classical economics', *Scottish Journal of Political Economy*, 8: 119–36.

Metcalfe, J.S. and Steedman, I. (1972) 'Reswitching and primary input use', *Economic Journal*, 82: 140–57.

—— (1973) 'Heterogeneous capital and the Heckscher-Ohlin-Samuelson theory of trade', in A.R. Nobay and M. Parkin (eds), *Essays in Modern Economics*, London: Macmillan.

Milgate, M. (1979) 'On the origin of the notion of "intertemporal equilibrium"', *Economica*, 44: 1–10.

Modigliani, F. (1944) 'Liquidity preference and the theory of interest and money', *Econometrica*, 12: 45–88.

—— (1963) 'The monetary mechanism and its interaction with real phenomena', *Review of Economics and Statistics*, 45: 79–107.

Momigliano, F. and Siniscalco, D. (1982) 'Note in tema di terzia-rizzazione e deindustrializzazione', *Moneta e Credito*, 138: 143–82.

—— (1984) 'Specializzazione internazionale, tecnologia e carat-teristiche dell'offerta', *Moneta e Credito*, 146: 121–66.

Montani, G. (1972) 'La teoria ricardiana della rendita', *L'industria*, 3–4: 221–43.

Naldi, N. (1998a) 'Some notes on Piero Sraffa's biography, 1917–27', *Review of Political Economy*, 10: 493–515.

—— (1998b) 'Sraffa a Perugia: novembre 1923–febbraio 1926', *History of Economic Ideas*, 6: 105–32.

—— (1998c) 'Dicembre 1922: Piero Sraffa e Benito Mussolini', *Rivista italiana degli economisti*, 3: 271–99.

—— (2000) "The friendship between Piero Sraffa and Antonio Gramsci in the years 1919 and 1927', *European Journal of the History of Economic Thought*, 7: 79–114.

Neumann, J. von (1945–46) 'A model of general economic equilibrium', *Review of Economic Studies*, 13: 1–9.

Newman, P. (1962) 'Production of commodities by means of commodities', *Schweizerische Zeitschrift für Volkswirtschaft und Statistik*, 98: 58–75.

Newman, P. and Vassilakis, S. (1988) 'Sraffa and imperfect competition', *Cambridge Journal of Economics*, 12: 37–42.

Panico, C. (1988a) *Interest and Profits in the Theories of Value and Distribution*, London: Macmillan.

—— (1988b) 'Sraffa on money and banking', *Cambridge Journal of Economics*, 12: 7–28.

Parrinello, S. (1970) 'Introduzione a una teoria neoricardiana del commercio internazionale', *Studi economici*, 25: 267–321.

—— (1977) 'Note sulla nozione di equilibrio nell'economia politica', *Giornale degli economisti*, 36: 3–24.

—— (1982a) 'Flexibility of choice and the theory of consumption', *Metroeconomica*, 34: 1–10.

—— (1982b) 'Some notes on monopoly, competition and the choice of techniques', *The Manchester School*, 52: 211–19.

Pasinetti, L.L. (1960) 'A mathematical formulation of the Ricardian system', *Review of Economic Studies*, 27: 78–98 (reprinted in Pasinetti 1974, *Growth and Income Distribution. Essays in Economic Theory*, Cambridge: Cambridge University Press).

—— (1962) 'Rate of profit and income distribution in relation to the rate of economic growth', *Review of Economic Studies*, 29: 267–79 (reprinted in Pasinetti 1974).

—— (1965) 'A new theoretical approach to the problems of economic growth', *Academiae Pontificiae Scientiarum Scripta Varia*, 28: 571–696.

—— (1966) 'Changes in the rate of profits and switches of techniques', *Quarterly Journal of Economics*, 80: 503–17.

—— (1969) 'Switches of technique and the "rate of return" in capital theory', *Economic Journal*, 79: 508–31.

—— (1970) 'Again on capital theory and Solow's "rate of return"', *Economic Journal*, 80: 428–31.

—— (1972) 'Reply to Mr. Dougherty', *Economic Journal*, 82: 1351–2.

—— (1973) 'The notion of vertical integration in economic analysis', *Metroeconomica*, 25: 1–29.

—— (1974) *Growth and Income Distribution. Essays in Economic Theory*, Cambridge: Cambridge University Press.

—— (1977a) *Lectures in the Theory of Production*, London: Macmillan.

—— (ed.) (1977b) *Contributi alla teoria della produzione congiunta*, Bologna: il Mulino.

—— (1979a) 'The unpalatability of the reswitching of techniques', *Revue d'économie politique*, 89: 637–42.

—— (1979b) 'The "unobtrusive postulate" of neoclassical economic theory', *Revue d'économie politique*, 89: 654–6.

—— (1981) *Structural Change and Economic Growth*, Cambridge: Cambridge University Press.

—— (1982) 'A comment on the "new view" of the Ricardian theory', in M. Baranzini (ed.), *Advances in Economic Theory*, Oxford: Blackwell.

—— (1984) 'The difficulty, and yet the necessity, of aiming at full employment: a comment on Nina Shapiro's Note', *Journal of Post Keynesian Economics*, 7: 246–8.

—— (1988) 'Growing subsystems, vertically hyper-integrated sectors and the labour theory of value', *Cambridge Journal of Economics*, 12: 125–34.

—— (1990) 'Sraffa's circular process and the concepts of vertical integration', in K. Bharadwaj and B. Schefold (eds).

—— (1993) *Structural Economic Dynamics*, Cambridge: Cambridge University Press.

Peach, T. (1984) 'David Ricardo's early treatment of profitability: a new interpretation', *Economic Journal*, 94: 733–51.

—— (1993) *Interpreting Ricardo*, Cambridge: Cambridge University Press.

Pivetti, M. (1991) *An Essay on Money and Distribution*, London: Macmillan.

Pollitt, B.H. (1988) 'The collaboration of Maurice Dobb in Sraffa's edition of Ricardo', *Cambridge Journal of Economics*, 12: 55–66.

Pownall, T. (1776) *A Letter from Governor Pownall to Adam Smith, L.L.D. F.R.S., Being an Examination of Several Points of Doctrine, Laid down in his "Inquiry into the Nature and Causes of the Wealth of Nations"*, London (reprinted in A. Smith 1977, *Correspondence*, edited by E.C. Mossner and I.S. Ross, Oxford: Oxford University Press).

Quinton, A. (1968) 'The later philosophy of Wittgenstein', in G. Pitcher (ed.), *Wittgenstein. A Collection of Critical Essays*, London: Macmillan.

Quadrio Curzio, A. (1967) *Rendita e distribuzione in un modello economico plurisettoriale*, Milan: Giuffrè.

—— (1975) *Accumulazione del capitale e reddito*, Bologna: il Mulino.

Quadrio Curzio, A. and Pellizzari, F. (1996) *Risorse, tecnologie, rendita*, Bologna: il Mulino.

Quadrio Curzio, A. and Scazzieri, R. (1984) 'Sui momenti costitutivi dell'economia politica', *Giornale degli economisti*, 43: 37–76.

Ranchetti, F. (1998) 'Sraffa e Keynes: note per una critica alla teoria keynesiana dell'interesse e della moneta', in N. De Vecchi and M.C. Marcuzzo (eds), *A cinquant'anni da Keynes*, Pavia: Edizioni Unicopli.

Ricardo, D. (1951–55) *Works and Correspondence*, edited by P. Sraffa, 10 vols, Cambridge: Cambridge University Press (vol. 11, *Indexes*, 1973).

Ridolfi, M. (1972) 'Aspetti del sistema teorico di Alfred Marshall. Una revisione critica di interpretazioni moderne', *Annali della Facoltà di scienze politiche, Università degli studi di Perugia*, XII, tomo 2°: 119–204.

Robertson, D. (1924) 'Those empty boxes', *Economic Journal*, 34: 16–30.

—— (1930) 'The trees of the forest', *Economic Journal*, 40: 80–9.

Robinson, J. (1933) *The Economics of Imperfect Competition*, London: Macmillan (2nd edition, 1969).

—— (1953) 'The production function and the theory of capital', *Review of Economic Studies*, 21: 81–106.

—— (1961) 'Prelude to a critique of economic theory', *Oxford Economic Papers*, 13: 53–8.

—— (1978) *Contributions to Modern Economics*, Oxford: Blackwell.

Roncaglia, A. (1978) *Sraffa and the Theory of Prices*, New York: Wiley (original Italian edn, 1975, *Sraffa e la teoria dei prezzi*, Rome-Bari: Laterza).

—— (1982) 'Hollander's Ricardo', *Journal of Post Keynesian Economics*, 4: 339–59.

—— (1983) 'Piero Sraffa: una bibliografia ragionata', *Studi economici*, 21: 137–66.

—— (1984) 'Sraffa e le banche', *Rivista milanese di economia*, 10: 104–12.

—— (1985) *Petty: the Origins of Political Economy*, Armonk: Sharpe.

—— (1988) 'Wage costs and employment: the Sraffian view', in J.A. Kregel, E. Matzner and A. Roncaglia (eds), *Barriers to Full Employment*, London: Macmillan.

—— (1990a) 'Le scuole sraffiane', in G. Becattini (ed.), *Il pensiero economico: temi, problemi e scuole*, Turin: Utet.

—— (1990b) 'Is the notion of long-period positions compatible with classical political economy?', *Political Economy*, 6: 103–11.

—— (1990c) 'Some remarks on the relevance of Sraffa's analysis for economic policy', in K. Bharadwaj and B. Schefold (eds), *Essays on Piero Sraffa*, London: Unwin Hyman (reprinted, London: Routledge, 1992).

—— (1991) 'Sraffa's 1925 article and Marshall's theory', *Quaderni di storia dell'economia politica*, 9: 373–97.

—— (1993) 'Toward a post-Sraffian theory of income distribution', *Journal of Income Distribution*, 3: 3–27.

—— (1995a) 'Introduzione', in A. Smith, *La ricchezza delle nazioni*, Rome: Newton.

—— (1995b) 'On the compatibility between Keynes's and Sraffa's viewpoints on output levels', in G. Harcourt, A. Roncaglia and

R. Rowley (eds), *Income and Employment in Theory and Practice*, London: Macmillan.

—— (1996) 'Why should economists study the history of economic thought?', *European Journal of the History of Economic Thought*, 3: 296–309.

Roncaglia, A. and Tonveronachi, M. (1978) 'Commenti a un recente studio di Modigliani e Padoa-Schioppa', *Moneta e Credito*, 121: 3–21.

—— (1985) 'The pre-Keynesian roots of the neoclassical synthesis', *Cahiers d'économie politique*, 10: 51–65.

Rosselli, A. (1985) 'The theory of the natural wage', in G. Caravale (ed.), *The Legacy of Ricardo*, Oxford: Blackwell.

Salvadori, N. (1979a) 'Mutamento dei metodi di produzione e produzione congiunta. Un commento al paragrafo 96 di "Produzione di merci a mezzo di merci"', *Studi economici*, 34: 79–94.

—— (1979b) 'Mutamento dei metodi di produzione e produzione congiunta', *Quaderni dell'istituto di economia*, Università degli studi di Siena, 6.

—— (ed.) (1981) *Esperimenti intellettuali ed economia politica*, Milan: Franco Angeli.

—— (1982) 'Existence of cost-minimizing systems within the Sraffa framework', *Zeitschrift für Nationalökonomie*, 42: 281–98.

—— (1985) 'Switching in methods of production and joint production', *The Manchester School*, 53: 156–78.

Salvadori, N. and Steedman, I. (eds) (1990) *Joint Production of Commodities*, Aldershot: Edward Elgar.

Samuelson, P.A. (1947) *Foundations of Economic Analysis*, Cambridge, MA: Harvard University Press.

—— (1948) *Economics*, New York: McGraw Hill.

—— (1962) 'Parable and realism in capital theory: the surrogate production function', *Review of Economic Studies*, 29: 193–206.

—— (1966) 'A summing up', *Quarterly Journal of Economics*, 80: 568–83.

—— (1971), 'Understanding the Marxian notion of exploitation: a summary of the so-called transformation problem between Marxian values and competitive prices', *Journal of Economic Literature*, 9: 399–431.

—— (1987) 'Sraffian economics', in J. Eatwell, M. Milgate and P. Newman (eds), *The New Palgrave. A Dictionary of Economics*, vol. 4, London: Macmillan.

Schefold, B. (1989) *Mr Sraffa on Joint Production and Other Essays*, London: Unwin Hyman.

—— (1997) *Normal Prices, Technical Change and Accumulation*, London: Macmillan.

Schumpeter, J.A. (1954) *History of Economic Analysis*, New York: Oxford University Press.

Screpanti, E. and Zenezini, M. (ed.) (1978) *Accumulazione del capitale e progresso tecnico*, Milan: Feltrinelli.

Shapiro, N. (1984) 'Involuntary unemployment in the long run: Pasinetti's formulation of the Keynesian argument – A review article', *Journal of Post Keynesian Economics*, 7: 235–45.

Shove, G.F. (1930) 'The representative firm and increasing returns', *Economic Journal*, 40: 94–116.

Solow, R.M. (1963) *Capital Theory and the Rate of Return*, Amsterdam: North Holland.

—— (1967) 'The interest rate and transition between techniques', in C.H. Feinstein (ed.), *Socialism, Capitalism and Economic Growth. Essays Presented to Maurice Dobb*, Cambridge: Cambridge University Press.

—— (1970) 'On the rate of return: reply to Pasinetti', *Economic Journal*, 80: 423–8.

Spaventa, L. (1968) 'Realism without parables in capital theory', in *Récherches récentes sur la fonction de production*, Centre d'études et de récherches universitaire de Namur.

Spriano, P. (1969) *Storia del Partito comunista italiano. Gli anni della clandestinità*, Turin: Einaudi.

—— (1970) *Storia del partito comunista italiano. I fronti popolari, Stalin, la guerra*, Turin:Einaudi.

—— (1977) *Gramsci in carcere e il partito*, Rome: Editori Riuniti.

Sraffa, P. (1920) *L'inflazione monetaria in Italia durante e dopo la guerra*, Milan: Scuola tipografica salesiana (reprinted in *Economia politica*, 1994, 11: 163–96).

—— (1922a) 'The bank crisis in Italy', *Economic Journal*, 32: 178–97 (reprinted in Sraffa 1986).

—— (1922b) 'L'attuale situazione delle banche italiane', *Manchester Guardian Commercial. La ricostruzione dell' Europa*, 7 December, 11: 694–5 (reprinted in Sraffa 1986).

—— (1923) 'Opinioni', *La rivoluzione liberale*, 16 October, 2: 128.

—— (1924) 'Obituary. Maffeo Pantaleoni', *Economic Journal*, 34: 648–53.

—— (1925) 'Sulle relazioni fra costo e quantità prodotta', *Annali di economia*, 2: 277–328 (reprinted in Sraffa 1986).

—— (1926) 'The laws of returns under competitive conditions', *Economic Journal*, 36: 535–50.

—— (1927) 'Due lettere a Tasca', *Stato operaio*, 1: 1089–95 (reprinted as *Il vero significato della 'quota 90'*, in L. Villari (ed.), *Il capitalismo italiano del Novecento*, Bari: Laterza, 1972: 180–91).

—— (1930) 'A criticism' and 'A rejoinder', in *Symposium on increasing returns and the representative firm*, *Economic Journal*, 40: 89–93.

—— (1932) 'Dr. Hayek on money and capital' and 'A rejoinder', *Economic Journal*, 42: 42–53, 249–51.

—— (1951) 'Introduction', in D. Ricardo, vol. 1.

—— (1960) *Production of Commodities by Means of Commodities*, Cambridge: Cambridge University Press.

—— (1962) 'Production of commodities: a comment', *Economic Journal*, 72: 477–9.

—— (1986) *Saggi*, edited by P. Garegnani, Bologna: il Mulino.

—— (1991) *Lettere a Tania per Gramsci*, edited by V. Gerratana, Rome: Editori Riuniti.

Steedman, I. (1977a) *Marx after Sraffa*, London: New Left Books.

—— (ed.) (1977b) *Teoria del commercio internazionale*, Bologna: Marsilio.

—— (ed.) (1979a) *Fundamental Issues in Trade Theory*, London: Macmillan.

—— (1979b) *Trade amongst Growing Economies*, Cambridge: Cambridge University Press.

—— (1980) 'Returns to scale and the switch in methods of production', *Studi economici*, 35: 5–13.

—— (1985a) 'Joint production and technical progress', *Political Economy*, 1: 41–52.

—— (1985b) 'Produced inputs and tax incidence theory', *Quaderni dell'Istituto di economia*, Università degli studi di Siena, 34.

—— (ed.) (1988) *Sraffian Economics*, 2 vols, Aldershot: Edward Elgar.

—— (1989) *From Exploitation to Altruism*, Cambridge: Polity Press.

—— (1992) 'Introduction', in P.H. Wicksteed, *The Co-ordination of the Laws of Distribution*, Aldershot: Edward Elgar.

Sylos Labini, P. (1954) 'Il problema dello sviluppo economico in Marx ed in Schumpeter', in G.U. Papi (ed.), *Teoria dello sviluppo economico*, Milan: Giuffrè (English transl. in Sylos Labini 1984: Chapter 2).

—— (1962) *Oligopoly and Technical Progress*, Cambridge, MA: Harvard University Press.

—— (1969) 'Introduzione di forme di mercato non concorrenziali nello schema di Sraffa e passaggio alla riproduzione allargata', mimeo, Rome.

—— (ed.) (1973) *Prezzi relativi e distribuzione del reddito*, Turin: Boringhieri.

—— (1974a) *Trade Unions, Inflation and Productivity*, Westmead: Saxon House.

—— (1974b) *Saggio sulle classi sociali*, Rome-Bari: Laterza.

—— (1977) 'Competition and economic growth in Adam Smith', in T. Wilson and A. Skinner (eds), *The Market and the State: Essays in Honour of Adam Smith*, Oxford: Oxford University Press (repr. in Sylos Labini, 1984: Chapter 1).

—— (1983) *Il sottosviluppo e l'economia contemporanea*, Rome-Bari: Laterza.

—— (1984) *The Forces of Economic Growth and Decline*, Cambridge, MA: MIT Press.

—— (ed.) (1994) *Carlo Marx: è tempo di un bilancio*, Rome-Bari: Laterza.

Togliatti, P. (ed.) (1962) *La formazione del gruppo dirigente del Partito comunista italiano*, Rome: Editori Riuniti.

Tonveronachi, M. (1983) *J.M. Keynes. Dall'instabilità ciclica all' equilibrio di sottoccupazione*, Rome: La Nuova Italia Scientifica.

—— (1991) 'Alcune considerazioni in tema di teorie finanziarie e processi di valorizzazione', in J.A. Kregel (ed.), *Nuove interpretazioni dell'analisi monetaria di Keynes*, Bologna: il Mulino.

Varri, P. (1974) 'Prezzi, saggio del profitto e durata del capitale fisso nello schema teorico di Piero Sraffa', *Studi economici*, 29: 5–44.

Vicarelli, S. (1975) 'Il "problema della trasformazione": fine di una controversia', *Note economiche*, 8: 91–138.

Wicksell, K. (1934) *Lectures on Political Economy*, vol. 1, *General Theory*, London, Routledge (original edn, 1901, *Forelasningar i nationalekonomi*, vol. 1, Stockholm-Lund: Fritzes-Berlingska).

—— (1936) *Interest and Prices*, London: Macmillan (original edn, 1898, *Geldzins und Guterpreise bestimmenden Ursachen*, Jena: G. Fischer).

Wittgenstein, L. (1922) *Tractatus Logico-Philosophicus*, London: Kegan Paul.

—— (1953) *Philosophische Untersuchungen (Philosophical Investigations)*, Oxford: Basil Blackwell.

Wright, G.H. von (1955) 'Ludwig Wittgenstein: a biographical sketch', *Philosophical Review*, 64 (reprinted in Malcolm, 1958).

Zaghini, E. (1967) 'Una nota sui subsistemi di Sraffa', *Studi economici*, 22: 290–305.

Index of names